SIBLING RIVALRY

Dr Richard C. Woolfson

· ·

SIBLING RIVALRY

Thorsons
An Imprint of HarperCollins*Publishers*

Thorsons
An Imprint of HarperCollins*Publishers*
77–85 Fulham Palace Road
Hammersmith, London W6 8JB
1160 Battery Street
San Francisco, California 94111–1213

Published by Thorsons 1995

10 9 8 7 6 5 4 3 2 1

A catalogue record for this book
is available from the British Library

ISBN 0 7225 3170 2

Printed in Great Britain by
HarperCollinsManufacturing Glasgow

In memory of my father

Contents

· · · · ·

Acknowledgements
· · · · ·

Thanks to Erica Smith
for help in preparing the final manuscript,
and to Lisa, Tessa and Eve
for their love and encouragement.

Introduction
· · · · ·

A few months ago I was invited to participate in a radio programme on the topic of 'sibling rivalry' – the normal jealousy that exists between children in the same family. As usual before a studio discussion of this sort, I asked our children (Tessa, then aged 14, and Eve, then aged 12) for their views on the subject. They have a close, friendly relationship, and we have not been unduly troubled by excessive bickering – though they have had their moments!

'Eve,' I innocently asked, when we were seated together for our evening meal. 'Why do you and Tessa sometimes fight with each other? Why are you sometimes jealous of each other?' Reasonable questions to ask a sensible adolescent, you would assume. However, I was surprised by her reply: 'That's not fair,' she retorted angrily. 'Why are you asking me? Why don't you ask Tessa?'

This sort of dialogue typifies sibling rivalry. It leaves parents with a you-can't-win feeling because a simple remark or an involuntary gesture can trigger or even intensify rivalry between the children. And what's so infuriating about sibling rivalry is that so often you can't really understand what your children are complaining about. To you, resources are divided fairly, but to your children the distribution (whether it be your love, time, clothes, money or toys) is inequitable.

Although you might expect sibling rivalry to diminish with age, in many instances it does not. If anything, it can become worse. I know of a brother and a sister, both in their early 50s with an age gap of two years between them, who still bicker over the quality of birthday presents they receive from their parents. Ridiculous as it may seem to outside observers, these two siblings still harbour grievances of inequality that stem from their childhood almost 50 years ago. Proof, indeed, that sibling rivalry can remain unresolved even in adulthood.

In this book the universality – and normality – of jealousy between brothers and sisters (or brothers and brothers, or sisters and sisters!) is explained. It cannot be eliminated altogether. But, as the book explains, there is lots that you can do to minimize it in your family. Magic solve-all recipes are not offered. However, useful strategies are fully discussed, and background theory and research findings are provided to give you a broader understanding of your children's development and of their emotional and psychological needs. This can help any parent with more than one child (irrespective of the age gap between them) or any parent who is even considering having at least two children.

1

· · · · ·

When Sibling Rivalry Begins: The Pregnancy

SECOND BABY

Right now, you have either got at least two children in your family, or you have got one child already and are pregnant with – or maybe contemplating – another. Perhaps you are one of those couples who have carefully planned the timing of the second pregnancy, so that upheaval to your way of life is kept to an absolute minimum (e.g. the baby is due later on in the year when your older children are back at school, or at the start of the year when it is the quiet season in your office so that you will not be badly missed during maternity leave). If so, then you will welcome the news with few anxieties.

However, perhaps you are one of those couples who were completely surprised when the pregnancy test proved positive, because you had not seriously considered having a second child just yet. Whether or not you expected the news about a second baby, the fact is that your life is about to change – hopefully, for the better! You will get over your amazement once the news sinks in.

Even at this point you can start to make arrangements and preparations that can help to reduce the effect of sibling rivalry later. After all, it stands to reason that if you are not entirely comfortable with the idea of having a new baby, then your older child is not going to be comfortable with the idea either – and that is unlikely to get the children's relationship off to a good start.

Ways to reduce sibling rivalry are available to you as soon as you become aware of the pregnancy.

IT IS DIFFERENT THIS TIME

Planned or not, the pregnancy, birth and upbringing of your next child will have a major impact on your lives. Coping with one young child is demanding enough – coping with two can seem an awesome challenge. And it will not just be a repeat of when your first child was a baby; things have changed. You are different.

Here are some reasons why parenthood is never the same the second time round:

- *Self-confidence.* Now that you have had the chance to turn your theories about child development into practice with your first baby, you are likely to be more confident and less anxious with the next one.
- *Priorities.* Bringing up your first child has given you a sense of perspective. Now you are better able to judge when an issue is important or trivial. For instance, you are probably less concerned with the minor details of child care (such as whether or not the colour of his trousers and jacket match perfectly), while being more aware of the responsibilities (such as providing him with love).
- *Privacy.* Having had a young child at home for a couple of years already, you have also adjusted to the reduction in your privacy as adults. The cry of a baby late in the evening when you have just gone to bed, or the patter of tiny feet on their way to your bedroom during the night counteracts even the strongest sexual urge. You

have become used to this potential disruption to your
sex life.

- *Your first child.* This time, baby makes four rather than
three. And your first child, even if only a toddler of
between 12 and 15 months, is more aware of the world
around him and of how changes at home affect him personally. Twelve months ago he would not have noticed
an extra 50 children in the house, but now the very
suggestion of a new baby gives him food for thought.

  Of course, your first child was not there when you
were pregnant the first time round, but now you will
have to consider his emotional needs, too. Much depends
on his age and personality. However, it is safe to assume
that more than ever he needs to be loved by you, to
feel respected and valued by you, and to feel safe and
secure with you.

- *Your family budget.* Two children are virtually twice as
costly as one. Although this may not be apparent when
they are very young (because of hand-me-down clothes
and baby-care equipment), increased costs are felt later,
when the oldest child is around three or four years old.
His appetite changes, his interests change, and daily
living expenses begin to rise significantly.

- *Organization.* Life with two pre-school children takes a
lot of planning and organization, and their routines may
be very different. A 'simple' five-minute trip to the local
shops can take hours if your baby is fast asleep and you
do not want to wake him early, or if your older child is
in the middle of toilet training and wets himself just as
you step out into the street.

- *Friends.* The people who know you well (such as friends
and relatives) will expect you to be a capable parent
during this pregnancy. They know that you have already
been through all the stages before, and so might not be
as supportive this time. Their excitement and support

13

that were stirred by the news of your first pregnancy will be less for the second one.

WHY HAVE ANOTHER CHILD?

The combination of these factors means that life with your second child will be unpredictable. No matter how much you expect him to be the same as your first, he will not be. Some couples are devastated, for instance, when they realize that although their first child was a very settled baby who quickly established a good sleeping and feeding routine, their second baby turns out to be fractious and constantly hungry. As with your first, it is a case of adapting to your second child's individual needs.

Anyway, you are not alone — statistics confirm that less than 25 per cent of couples only have one child, and an increasing number of couples have three or more children. So life with several children cannot be that bad, despite the increased opportunities for sibling rivalry in larger families! Never let the thought of sibling rivalry put you off having more than one child.

Many couples who already have one child want to increase their family size because they are worried about the **effects of being an only child**. There is a popular belief that all only children are spoiled, precocious, comfortable with adults but not with children, and always want to be the centre of attention (although this is rarely the case in reality). The fear of having a child like this encourages parents to consider a brother or sister for him. In addition, there is the obvious practical factor that an only child does not have other children at home to play with. Of course, he can invite friends round to the house to play, but that is not the same as a having a sibling there every day. Perhaps this was a consideration for you.

And despite being a free and more liberal society, having only one child is still not the norm. Your **friends and relatives assume you will have another baby** in due course because they did when they were in that situation. Social pressure to increase family size can wear down the patience of the most determined mum and dad. Statements from other people such as 'You must be thinking about having a brother for him now that he's two,' 'I think it's time you gave us another grandchild' or 'Is there something wrong that you've only got one child?' undoubtedly create pressure on you to fulfil these expectations.

There are couples who are determined to have at least one boy and one girl in their family. Rightly or wrongly, they want to have **'one of each'**, 'a matching set', and they are prepared to continue conceiving until this goal is achieved. The difficulty with this strategy is that the focus is on the sex of the second and subsequent children (and suppose the first three or four are all the same sex?), not on the individual qualities of the child. In the long term, the couple may never be able to shed their disappointment that, say, the second child was not a girl, and this may affect their relationship with him.

Far better to have a second child for **positive reasons**, which might be that you simply enjoy looking after babies and young children, that you enjoy being with them and that you enjoy their company. There is nothing wrong in liking parenthood! Just because your best friend was desperate for her babies to become more independent so that she could return to work does not mean that you have to feel the same way. If you make a conscious choice to expand your family size for this reason, then that creates a good attitude towards your second child even during the pregnancy – and this positive outlook will rub off on your first child.

HOW THE SECOND PREGNANCY AFFECTS YOU

Even before the new baby arrives, your attitudes, actions and behaviour about your second pregnancy will influence the perceptions your older child has of the impending arrival. For instance, if you complain constantly about how tired you are because of the pregnancy, then this increases the likelihood that your older child will harbour negative feelings towards his sibling even before the birth. The same effect will be achieved if your partner regularly bemoans the increased expenditure that the second baby will incur and the negative impact that this will have on your family life.

So this time round you have to think about your firstborn child as well as yourself and your partner. However, you have the advantage of knowing roughly what lies ahead of you. You have been through it all before, you have met the nurses, doctors and medical staff, you have been to the antenatal classes and you probably recall your way around the maternity hospital. This knowledge and previous experience usually work in your favour, as you will not have a first-time parent's fear of the unknown. Tension is lower, confidence is higher.

Yet having been through it all before can also work against you. For instance, if the first pregnancy was tiresome, if the delivery was traumatic for you or your partner, or if the postnatal period proved to be painful and unpleasant, then you may not look forward to the second pregnancy with such eager anticipation. On the contrary, you might dread going through it all again.

Remember, though, that each pregnancy is unique; the second time round may bear little if any resemblance to the first. For example, if morning sickness was a big problem with the first pregnancy, the second may be completely free of it (or vice versa). However, both mother and father will probably need more rest this time round because life is more hectic – the first time you did not have a baby to feed, amuse, wash and put to sleep as well.

The same health considerations apply to your second pregnancy as they did to your first. The damaging effects on the foetus of cigarettes, alcohol and drugs are well documented. Your baby will be adversely affected, and the effects can be permanent. Many women find that pregnancy is sufficient motivation to give up smoking altogether.

The delivery process generally takes less time with a second baby. There are two factors causing this: First, the amount of time the mother spends in labour with a second child will usually be shorter; it is as though her body has learned from the first birth and is able to take her through the second birth at a faster pace. On average, subsequent labours take only around six or seven hours, whereas first labours are often twice that length of time. Second, medical and nursing staff expect 'more experienced' mums to leave the hospital much sooner than first-timers. The recovery process takes less time, parents tend to adjust to the new baby more quickly, and the staff know that you already have experience caring for a young baby.

TAKING CARE OF YOURSELF

If you feel tired, irritable and stressed – particularly in the later stages of the second pregnancy, when your first child knows a young brother or sister is on the way – then this will contaminate your first child's attitude towards the new arrival. The chart below offers tips for coping successfully with a second pregnancy:

Suggestion	What to do
Sleep	Pregnant mums need as much sleep as they can get – being pregnant makes you tired. Whenever you have a few moments free, settle into a chair or on the bed, close your eyes and let yourself nod off. You will feel better for it.
Plan	Time is at a premium, given the average woman's usual daily schedule, new set of hospital and clinic appointments, and reduction in energy levels during pregnancy. Try to plan your day as best you can so that you do not feel overwhelmed by all you have to do.
Delegate	If your partner does not already help around the house, now is the time to change things. He has to play his part – even if only for the duration of the pregnancy – so that the strain on you is eased. Perhaps your health visitor can persuade him if you cannot.
Accept	The chances are that people will help you, perhaps by doing some of your shopping for you or by looking after your older child for a few hours so that you can have a break on your own. Do not feel guilty about accepting these offers of support.
Ask	You do not have to prove that you are the most capable pregnant mother in living memory. It is perfectly acceptable to feel and look as though you are struggling. If you feel you need help, just ask. At worst your request will be denied, that is all.
Think	Your second pregnancy is difficult for your first child, too, although in different ways. He still needs time with mum and dad, time that he can call his own, time when you and he can be together. Make a big effort to have a few

	minutes with him each day.
Share	Despite your experience of pregnancy and birth, you are bound to have occasional worries and anxieties during this pregnancy too. Do not bottle them up inside because you think people expect you to be confident – share them with your partner.

THE EFFECT OF THE AGE GAP

The age gap between your first child and second child is one factor that affects the level of sibling rivalry between them. The age difference also has an effect on you and your partner. Every child is an individual, and every couple is unique. However, there are findings from psychological research regarding the relationship between different age gaps and their impact on the family. Remember that these findings signify trends, not certainties, and never attempt to plan your family spacing solely in the hope of avoiding some of the negative aspects.

When the Age Gap is Less Than 24 Months:

- There is a strong chance that your children will grow up to be good friends. Although the age difference is marked in early childhood, a gap of less than two years becomes less significant later on as they begin to share interests.
- Your first child is still quite young during your second pregnancy, and is therefore less aware of what is going on. He still needs your love and reassurance, but he will not be as insecure as an older child might be.
- If you have taken off a lot of time with your first baby from your career, having another relatively soon may leave you with no time to re-establish yourself at work.

The thought of taking a further break from your career, so close to the previous break, may cause you some concern about your future job prospects.

- If you are the mother, you may not have fully recovered from any health difficulties you experienced as a result of the birth. The stress of the second pregnancy so close to the first could reactivate previous physical problems.

When the Age Gap Is Between 24 and 48 Months:

- His daily schedule is different from the baby's routine. He stays up later than the baby, eats different foods and enjoys different toys. This makes him feel more grown-up and he will probably like the role of 'big brother'.
- As your older child has outgrown all of his baby clothes and no longer uses baby-care equipment such as a cot, baby walker, etc., you will not have to buy so many new things for your new baby.
- Your older child's increased understanding means that he is more likely to feel threatened by the new baby. He knows that the baby will take your attention away from him, and sibling rivalry may be strong as a result.
- When you are feeding the baby, your older child may be very jealous at that precise moment because he sees you both in such close physical contact. He may push the baby away or try to snuggle between you.

When the Age Gap Is More than 48 Months:

- You will have lots of time to spend with your new baby because your older child will be at school full-time now. Similarly, you can organize your day to have time available for your older child when he arrives home – so jealousy is reduced.

- Your older child's after-school activities can continue without too much interruption because he is more independent. For instance, he will not mind taking a lift from his friend's mum; getting there is what matters most to him.
- Your older child can show off about his new brother or sister to his friends, like a new toy. They will be delighted and this will make him feel happier. His class teacher will make a big fuss of him when she hears the news.
- Getting used to having a new baby in the house can be difficult for you, having had a long break from changing nappies, baby feeds, and so on. You will adapt soon enough, but you may be exhausted at first.

When There Is an Age Gap of 10 Years or More:

- You need have no concerns about sibling rivalry. Your older child is so mature and confident that the presence of a young baby at home does not bother him at all. He will be proud of his younger sibling.
- Instead of just having two sets of helping hands to care for the baby, you will have three, because your older child will want to become involved, too. The novelty may wear off in time, but he will take part in caring for the baby.
- There is a risk that your first child may spoil his little brother or sister – that is part of the pleasure of being a much older sibling. Keep a watchful eye on the situation so that you can monitor it closely.
- Most of your friends have long forgotten what it means to have a young baby in the house. They may not be entirely sympathetic when you start talking about baby issues, or if you have a problem getting a babysitter for an evening.

SUMMARY

A second child affects family life, possibly more dramatically than first time round because this time there is an existing child to consider. Everyone has to make adjustments during the pregnancy — the mother has to make sure she takes good care of herself, the father has to make sure he helps, and the child has to get used to a mum and dad who are more tired than they usually are. If your child is given his fair share of attention at this stage, then he will not start to develop a negative attitude towards the new arrival.

The age gap between your existing child and second child affects the level of sibling rivalry between them, although every child is an individual. Different age gaps have different effects on you and your partner, and on your child. It is worth being aware of these effects, but remember that they are only trends, not certainties — so never attempt to plan your family spacing solely in the hope of avoiding some of the negative possibilities.

2
· · · · ·

When Sibling Rivalry Begins:
The Birth

BREAKING THE NEWS

The way that you break the news of the pregnancy can affect
your older child's adjustment to the new family member. The
baby is part of her life − it is not only you and your partner
who will have to adapt to change. Clearly, you want your
elder child to feel positive and happy about her future brother or sister right from the first moment, but this does not
always happen. Some children react very badly, perhaps
by ignoring the information completely or by throwing a
tantrum.

Here are some factors to consider when breaking the news
of the pregnancy to your elder child:

- *You tell, not someone else.* She has a right to know about
  the baby before other people hear about it. Of course,
  you will probably tell your close friends and relatives
  first, but do not leave it too long before you tell your
  child − she may overhear snatches of conversation, put
  two and two together, and then be very annoyed and
  worried because you have not said anything about it to
  her.
- *Timing.* There is never a 'perfect' moment to tell your
  child. However, she does not need to know immediately.
  You (or your partner) may be feeling unwell with

23

morning sickness for the first few months, so if possible do not tell her until you are feeling more robust physically. But you cannot leave it much beyond the fourth or fifth month, because she will see that Mum's tummy is growing.

- *Style.* Try to be relaxed and smiling when you announce the pregnancy to your elder child. Tell her straight out that she is going to have a new brother or sister in a few months, and add that they are both going to get on well with each other. You can also say that babies love having an elder sister, which means that the baby will adore her.

- *Child's age.* The exact wording of your comments depends, of course, on your elder child's age. A toddler of 18 months may not fully understand what you tell her (and you may have to repeat it later), whereas a child aged 4 or 5 years may need a bit more than just the basic information (such as what will happen to her when the new baby comes home).

- *Child's reaction.* Do not underestimate the effect that this news can have on your elder child. She may think that your having another child is a sign that you do not love her as much — after all, she reckons, if there was nothing wrong with her then why would you need a second child? Watch her face very closely when you tell her, to monitor her reaction.

- *Be flexible.* If you see that she becomes uncomfortable as you speak to her about the new baby, stop for a moment to check out her feelings. For instance, you might say 'There is lots more to talk about but I can see you look worried. Why is that?' This lets her know that you want her to share her feelings with you, and that you care about her.

- *Questions.* She will probably want to ask you lots of questions, usually about the way the new baby might affect her life. For instance, she may want to know where her sibling will sleep, and whether or not she will still be able to have a bedroom of her own. Most of her concerns at this stage will be practical – give her the reassurance that she needs.

- *Accepting.* Whatever her reaction, make sure that she does not feel rejected by you. It would be wonderful if she were overjoyed at the thought of a little brother or sister, but the chances are that her immediate reaction will be more self-interested. That is perfectly normal. Do not be disappointed with her because she is not overjoyed; accept her response, whatever it is.
- *Repetition.* Children have the habit of asking the same questions over and over again, even though you have told her the answers several times before. This is a child's way of coming to terms with the information contained in the answer. So try not to be annoyed with her when she asks you for the umpteenth time whether or not you will like the baby more than her.

THE BIRTH ITSELF

There will be a change in your family's usual routine when you go into hospital for the second delivery. Well in advance, explain to your elder child that when she was born Mum went into hospital to be cared for, and that the same will happen with this baby. She will be concerned about three things:

First, who will look after her while Mum is in hospital. She wants to know the arrangements (e.g., that Dad will look after her, or that she will be staying with a grandparent). She needs to know where she will be staying and who will be caring for her.

25

Second, how much disruption there will be to her routine. She will be happier if she can continue attending nursery each day, or continue going to her dance classes, despite the fact that mum is in hospital.

Third, how long Mum will be away. Your elder child has probably never thought about Mum in relation to hospitals before. Make an educated guess about the probable length of stay in the maternity hospital (e.g. four days), add on an extra day for good measure, and then reassure your older child that 'Mum will be back on Friday.'

If you cover these essential points, your elder child will be less anxious about the impending birth.

Some parents want their elder child to be present at the birth itself. Indeed, there are many documented cases in which the baby has been delivered at home because there was no time to reach the maternity hospital, allowing the elder child to witness the whole event. Parents who have had this experience often report how it has brought them all closer together as a family.

A recent psychological study compared differences in sibling rivalry between children who were present at and those who were absent from the birth of a sibling. Parents were asked questions about aspects of their child's behaviour that could be caused by sibling rivalry (such as babyish behaviour, temper tantrums, taking toys from the baby, saying she does not like her new baby, nightmares, sleeping difficulties and aggression towards mum and dad). The results showed that there were no significant differences between the two groups of children regarding these dimensions of behaviour. The research evidence, therefore, is inconclusive, and the presence of an elder child at the birth of a younger brother or sister remains an individual decision for the parents.

You have a right to exercise choice when it comes to birth arrangements, in conjunction with the professionals supporting the ante-natal care. But think carefully about the elder child's perception of the birth. If she sees mum in pain and discomfort caused by labour and the delivery – even though you know that childbirth is a natural process – then she may have negative feelings towards her new sibling. It is something that should be thought out very carefully.

THE FIRST MEETING

Now that your baby has arrived safe and well into the world, and you and your partner have had an opportunity to speak to each other after the birth, you have to arrange for your elder child to visit her new sibling for the first time. **Plan this carefully.** Handled well, this can start their relationship off on a good note, but handled badly it can set their relationship off on a sour note.

You and your partner will have arranged a specific time for your older child to visit you. When she arrives, she wants Mum to look well, as this will confirm everything is fine. However, **she may be a little remote** because she is subdued and confused by the hospital surroundings, and she may not immediately rush over to hug mum. Do not be upset by this, she is only being shy. Give her a big hug, tell her how pleased Mum is to see her, before you even mention the baby. Ask her how she is, what she has been doing, and so on. In other words, **make her the centre of attention**.

After a few minutes, show her the baby (hopefully, sleeping soundly in the cot). Take her hand as she walks gingerly over to see him. Explain that **the baby has a present for her**, and that it is in the cot beside him. She will be thrilled about this, even though she might not be prepared to admit it at the time. Then hand her a present that she can give to the baby. Young children are very practical and easily influenced – swapping presents like this helps her view the new baby very positively.

27

Your elder child may want to stroke the baby's cheek, or hold him gently. Let her do this. Although she suddenly seems huge compared to her sibling, **she will not cause him any harm by touching him**. If she does want to hold him in her arms, then you can have your arms round her too, to make her feel more secure.

Your elder child might make unflattering comments about the marks on his face, the size of his head, the colour of his hair, and so on. Let her say these things, without being defensive.

JEALOUSY BACK HOME

The chart below lists some suggestions for reducing sibling rivalry during the first few weeks back home, when your family is once again reunited:

Suggestion	What To Do
Accept her feelings	You may be sad when you see your elder child's difficult behaviour in these early stages. But her anger or aggressiveness, her sullenness or loudness, are all normal reactions, stemming from her sense of insecurity. She will settle down in time.
Do not fuss	Although your elder child has to adjust to sharing your attention with the baby, she needs time to get used to it. So, if possible, try not to fuss too much about your new baby in front of your elder child, or feelings of resentment and isolation may result.
Give her tasks	She will feel less remote from her

28

new sibling if she can participate in his routine. Even though you can do all the basic chores yourself, ask your elder child, for instance, to put the used tissue in the waste-paper basket, or to fetch a clean towel from the cupboard.

Family trips Get life back to normal as soon as possible. Going out with a young child and a baby is never easy and requires lots of preparation, but it is worth the effort. Potential feelings of hostility towards the new arrival are reduced when there is minimal disruption to family life.

Attention Give her attention, even though it may not be convenient for you or your visitors. Elder children tend to be pushed aside by the stampede of well-wishers who come to the house to see the new baby. If possible, have a word with prospective visitors and suggest they bring a small gift for her as well.

Quality time Remember that your elder child needs to feel that she is special in your life. Make time to talk to her every day, to listen to her news and to hear about anything she wants to tell you. She will be less jealous of the baby when she realizes you still have time for her.

SUMMARY

Tell your child beforehand that she is going to have a new baby brother or sister, probably around the fifth or sixth month. Her reaction to the news could vary from happiness to tears. Listen to her and accept her reaction, whatever it is. Some parents like their elder child to be present at the actual delivery, but that is a personal decision.

The first meeting between elder child and baby can be made easier by swapping gifts with each other. And when the family are together at home again, there are many ways of reducing sibling rivalry, such as involving the elder child in the care of the new baby, giving her individual attention too, and keeping to the normal family routine whenever possible.

3

. . . . .

Sibling Rivalry:
Ages and Stages

CHANGES

Sibling rivalry will probably be present at every stage of your children's lives, no matter how young or old they are. (Of course, when they are adults you can leave them to sort it out themselves, whereas you have to become actively involved as peacemaker when they are children). However, the way this rivalry is expressed changes as the children grow older.

The list below outlines the typical ways in which jealousy between the children in a family is expressed. Bear in mind, though, that it depends largely on the children's individual personalities, the age of the children and the age difference between them, and the way they are managed at home by their parents. The examples given may not mirror your own children exactly, but the chances are that you will recognize some aspects reflected in their relationships. The suggestions offered for helping reduce sibling rivalry at each stage are developed more fully in the next chapter.

18 MONTHS
Development

The child is at a very egocentric stage of development, in which he is not very aware of the presence of others around him. If he is in the company of other children (for example at playgroup) he will tend to play on his own, not co-operating with the others and probably not even glancing in their direction. Being able to walk about without support gives him a strong feeling of independence. This feeling shows through in other areas as well, and he may try to manage his own feeding, take his own socks and shoes off, and try to open and shut doors without help. Despite this, a child at this stage of development can be very clingy to his parents at times.

How Rivalry Manifests at this Age

a) He is the elder child: Sibling rivalry tends to be at a minimum, because he is so focused on himself and his own needs. His attention will be drawn to his younger sister mostly when she starts to cry. However, as long as he does not experience much change at home, then he will not show strong resentment towards her.

b) He is the younger child: A child aged 18 months does not represent much of a threat to older siblings, and so sibling rivalry is not usually a difficulty at this time. If he does find his way to the other children's toys or games, they will be able to use their bigger size and coordination to their advantage.

How You Can Help

Your intervention might not be needed much at present. Nevertheless, you should encourage your children to respect each other's property. Point out to your elder child that the younger one does not yet understand not to touch things that are not his. He will learn this in time.

2 YEARS
Development

A child of this age is often full of his own self-importance. When he wants something, he wants it immediately — and he does not like being told 'No.' Temper tantrums are common because the child is easily frustrated and his tolerance is limited. In time he will learn that family life involves give and take, but for the moment he becomes furious when his wishes are blocked. Because he is much more agile now, he stomps about when he is annoyed, or perhaps he lies on the floor screaming. Toilet training usually starts around now.

How Sibling Rivalry Manifests at this Age

a) He is the elder child: A typical 2-year-old is alert enough to know that the presence of a younger brother or sister will have an impact on his life at home. He will not notice the effect immediately, but he may become attention-seeking or babyish himself when, for instance, he sees the new baby being fed.

b) He is the younger child: Because he is at a peak level of curiosity, he likes to explore into rooms and cupboards, even those that are not his. This can be very annoying for older brothers and sisters, who will not be pleased to find the contents of their wardrobe strewn chaotically across the bedroom floor.

How You Can Help

It is important for you to establish, and maintain, a consistent family discipline. Your toddler may not like rules that put restrictions on some aspects of his behaviour — but he will get used to them eventually. Be prepared to hold your

33

ground when he has a temper tantrum because he cannot play with his sibling's toys.

3 YEARS
Development

He has a greater level of independence and is able to do more himself, such as dressing and undressing, using cutlery at mealtimes and attending to himself in the toilet. The child's increased use of language means that he is now talking in 3- or 4-word sentences; he can communicate his feelings and ideas more accurately using words rather than temper tantrums. However, he can be moody and impatient if things do not go his way all the time – a peaceful afternoon can be turned almost instantly into argument. Three-year-olds begin to build their own world and can become territorial, especially about books, toys and clothes.

How Sibling Rivalry Manifests at this Age

a) He is the elder child: An age gap of three years between a child and his younger brother or sister is associated with the peak level of sibling rivalry, largely because the child is old enough and mature enough to understand that a new baby will draw attention and resources away from him. He anticipates this, before he sees evidence of it.

b) He is the younger child: Elder siblings are able to spell out the rules of family life more clearly, and he will co-operate more than before – although he remains self-interested and determined. The 3-year-old may be invited to join in games with his older sister, but arguments are likely because he cannot yet follow rules.

How You Can Help

Reassure the child that he is loved as much as any other child in the family, whether he is the elder or younger sibling. He will start to listen to explanations of this nature. Encourage your children to play together if the age gap is not too great, and offer guidance on how they could co-operate with each other.

4 YEARS
Development

A child of this age is lively, imaginative and desperate to understand everything that goes on around him. Self-confidence improves; he takes great delight in trying to master climbing frames, swings and balancing logs. A 4-year-old has begun to play co-operatively with other children. He accepts the need to share and to take turns. Even so, he can quickly lose his temper when playing, but is less likely to storm off in a huff. He also begins to show a sense of humour. The child takes an interest in helping round the house, and may want to help you.

How Sibling Rivalry Manifests at this Age

a) He is the elder child: He accepts the reality that there is a new baby in the family, but he will not be entirely happy about it. At times he might be mean to the new-born, often not intentionally. For instance, his loving hug might become too enthusiastic and the baby ends up screaming in discomfort.
b) He is the younger child: He probably shows great loyalty to his older brothers or sisters, and may even follow them around like a faithful puppy. On the other hand,

there will be times when he forcefully attempts to boss his older siblings about, and gets angry and aggressive when they do not do as he says.

How You Can Help

Be ready to intervene when bickering begins. Keep a careful watch when he is playing with the young baby, and try not to leave them alone together unsupervised if it can be avoided. Explain to him that just as he has rights of privacy, so too have his older brother and/or sister.

5 YEARS
Development

Starting school is the big step at this stage of development. It signifies a new transition in the child's life, in which he perceives himself as 'a big boy'. This separates him distinctly from any younger siblings. At the same time, however, his self-confidence is very fragile. He can become easily upset if he thinks others his own age are more capable than him at school. He will have genuine affection for other members of his family, but should be able to separate well from mum and dad each day when he goes to the infant class. A 5-year-old is usually protective towards younger children, and will comfort one who is upset.

How Sibling Rivalry Manifests at this Age

a) He is the elder child: He feels good about himself because he is now at school, and is perhaps more tolerant of his younger sibling. However, he may try to dominate the younger one, telling her what to do and how to do it – this inevitably results in conflict.

b) He is the younger child: He wants to be like his older siblings, perhaps wanting to walk with them to school – and he may not understand why they prefer to go with their own friends. The achievements of the older children in the family can cause him anxiety, particularly if he feels that he is not as capable.

How You Can Help

Boost his self-confidence whenever you can by praising his achievements and by taking an interest in his work at school (or nursery, if he has not yet started school). This reduces his desire to compete with others in the family. Encourage him to take help from his older brothers or sisters when they think they have an answer to his questions.

6 YEARS
Development

Friendships become important at this stage in a child's life, although most 6-year-olds still change their friendships reasonably regularly because they do not have the maturity or commitment to sustain peer relationships. Another characteristic of a child this age is a willingness to tell others what they should do in a specific situation, even though he does not always follow his own advice. Comparisons with other children become increasingly important – he wants to achieve at least as well as they do, and shows distress if he cannot reach that standard. Confrontations – both verbal and physical – are common among 6-year-olds.

How Sibling Rivalry Manifests at this Age

a) He is the older child: Tolerance of younger brothers and sisters is at a premium; the child has his own ideas, his

37

own likes and dislikes and he does not react well to the intrusions of younger siblings. He may try to use the age gap as a way of manipulating and controlling the younger ones in the family.

b) He is the younger child: He will begin to respect the rights of the other children in the family, and realize the reciprocity of relationships (for example, if he is nice to his older sister, the chances are that she will be nice to him). The child will now openly voice his anxieties if he thinks he is being treated unfairly.

How You Can Help

Treat him seriously. If he complains that you treat him differently from the way you treat your other children, listen to his views, then explain your side of the story. Discourage him from raising his hands against his siblings when he is in dispute with them; stress that discussion is the preferred means of solving a disagreement.

7–8 YEARS
Development

He will not be as quiet as he was before. The rough-and-tumble of school life – coupled with his realization that he is no longer the infant he once was – tends to make him more outgoing. He enjoys playing with friends, and may have one or two close friends with whom he spends most of his time. Siblings, both older and younger, can be a bit of a nuisance for him because they may interfere with the smooth running of his life. He is very aware of who gets what and he may be very insistent that, for instance, sweets are shared out exactly. The child resents the fact that he gets 'hand-me-down' clothes from his older brother – he wants new clothes.

How Sibling Rivalry Manifests at this Age

a) He is the older child: He beings to perceive himself as 'older'. While he is naturally protective towards younger siblings, he does not want to have to be responsible for them whenever they play together outside. The antics of a younger brother or sister may annoy him if he is with his friends.

b) He is the younger child: He looks up to his older siblings, as long as there is an age gap of at least two years or so. Less than that and the competition may be fierce; more than that and neither is a threat to each other and the 7- to 8-year-old will take pride in his older brother's or sister's achievements.

How You Can Help

Avoid comparing your children with each other — a sure recipe for disaster. No child likes a comparison with a sibling, whether or not that comparison puts him in a favourable light. Let the children develop their own individual interests, rather than expecting them to follow in each other's footsteps.

9–10 YEARS
Development

Physical appearance is very important to children of this age. Although not quite adolescents they are very conscious of having the right clothes for the right occasion. And nothing you can say or do will convince a 9- or 10-year-old that the clothes he has are perfectly suitable if he thinks they are not. Hand in hand with this comes an increased sensitivity and vulnerability; he is easily upset by a negative comment from brothers or sisters. Despite a more even and relaxed temperament, he becomes angry very quickly when little siblings annoy him. His bedroom is now out of bounds to everyone – except mum and dad.

How Sibling Rivalry Manifests at this Age

a) He is the older child: He cares deeply for his younger brother or sisters, and tries to guide them whenever he can – but he will have no patience when they do not do as he says. He will be irritated by their mischief, yet he will defend them against aggression from others.
b) He is the younger child: The child treats his older siblings with respect. He likes his privacy and therefore respects their privacy too. At times he will try to take part in some of their activities, if the age gap is not too great, and he will probably be very well-behaved on these occasions.

How You Can Help

Remind him that he was a young child only a few years ago, and that he should be more patient with the younger children in the family. He may on the other hand need to be reminded that his older siblings need their own personal space. Boost his self-esteem by telling him how well he is getting on at school and at home.

11–12 YEARS
Development

The child's peer group matters more than anything else and is now the biggest influence on his attitudes, clothes and general behaviour. To be accepted by his friends he must do what they do, wear what they wear, and share similar ideas. Siblings of all ages become less significant in his life. In particular, he is not so influenced by his older brothers or sisters. He will resent being told by others in the family that his clothes do not look very nice, because as far as he is concerned they are the height of fashion. He wants a higher level of independence, more choices in his life and more involvement in day-to-day decisions.

How Sibling Rivalry Manifests at this Age

a) He is the older child: The fierce independence shown by an 11- or 12-year-old means that he has difficulty getting on with the other children in the family. He may have little time for the younger ones, treating them with sarcasm and imitating them when they complain about something. He is too interested in his friends to care much about his siblings.

b) He is the younger child: His adulation of older brothers and sisters fades as his confidence and independence increases. Their styles and fashions are unlikely to be his, and as a result he may reject their advice and suggestions. He is often convinced that no one in the family is prepared to listen to his point of view.

How You Can Help

Do not dismiss his moans and groans simply as 'the teenage years'. He is developing his own identity, his own self-image, and part of that process necessarily means rejecting the values of others in the family — so avoid taking his negative behaviour personally. Be patient with him, if possible.

13–14 YEARS
Development

Two personality trends often dominate the adolescent's life. First, he has an increased interest in opposite-sex friendships. Of course the intensity of this varies from child to child, but most adolescents of this age are more aware of the opposite sex than ever before. Second, he is convinced that he knows all the answers. At times he may be so self-confident about his own perceived wisdom that he openly rejects any alternative perspective. He exerts greater control over his life and is prepared to argue his claims, such as when he wants to stay out an extra hour at the weekends, or wants to go to a rock concert on his own.

How Sibling Rivalry Manifests at this Age

a) He is the older child: Much depends on the age gap. He probably gets on very well with a brother or sister who is still a pre-schooler – he will not feel threatened by the younger sibling and will be affectionate towards him. With a smaller age gap he may be unwittingly rude to the younger child on occasions.

b) He is the younger child: Since he treats his older brother or sister with respect – because he is greatly interested in their activities and wants to learn from someone who is older – relationships are good. Sibling rivalry is rarely a major problem at this stage of development.

How You Can Help

There is not much to be done now. The effort you put in during the previous years should have paid off, and the bickering that marked earlier family life will be less intense.

Conflicts can usually be resolved reasonably quickly. However, there are occasions when you have to remind your child to be less harsh with his comments.

IT IS NOT ANY EASIER HAVING AN ONLY CHILD

Looking at the development of sibling rivalry from birth through adolescence, there is no doubt that the greatest stress point is during the pre-school years. From then on, conflict between your children starts to fade in intensity until it has almost – but not completely – fizzled out towards the end of adolescence.

Things get easier as your children get older – always reassuring to know! And it is worth reminding yourself that having only one child also brings challenges. An only child can turn out to be quite a handful, because of the following factors:

- he is always centre-stage in the family;
- he never has to get used to sharing;
- he has mum and dad all to himself;
- he spends most of his leisure time with grown-ups;
- he may be spoiled by his parents.

These factors mean that parents of an only child have to work very hard to ensure that he does not grow up to be selfish or anti-social. He may have difficulties when it comes to getting on with others his own age, and there may be lots of fights and arguments because he is so used to getting his own way. Of course, the effect of these possible pitfalls can be greatly reduced by the child's parents – just as sibling rivalry can be reduced by concerned and sensitive parents – but that is as demanding as coping with squabbling between children.

SUMMARY

Sibling rivalry can be found during most stages of childhood, and is something all parents should expect. It tends to peak during the pre-school years, though starts to reduce from then on. There are things you can do at each stage of your children's development to minimize the impact of sibling rivalry. Some parents are tempted to have only one child, but this family structure simply poses its own, though different, challenges.

4

. . . . .

How to Control It

'IT'S NOT FAIR'

You cannot win, no matter how hard you try. Even if one of your children has been ill in bed for several days and you buy her a comic to cheer her up, chances are that your other children will accuse you of being unfair! And you can reason with your other children until you are blue in the face – your action will still be construed as a sign of inequality in family life. None of your children is immune to this type of rivalry.

However, although you cannot eliminate sibling rivalry altogether (even by following the suggestions given in the previous chapters), you can attempt to control it. Do not leave it all to chance. The chart below outlines key factors – within your control – which directly influence the level of sibling rivalry in your family.

Factor	Significance
Treating children seriously	Your children must feel they are respected by you and that you take their feelings seriously. Sibling rivalry intensifies when the children feel their parents are not prepared to listen.
Avoiding comparisons	No child likes to be compared

to her older or younger siblings. Comparisons are divisive and drive a wedge between brothers and sisters – someone always loses out in comparisons.

Fairness, not equality
A major source of jealousy between children in a family is the belief that resources are not distributed fairly. Sibling rivalry ferments when unfairness is perceived to exist.

Change without criticism
Too often parents get trapped in a rut of criticism because of the strain of perpetual bickering among the children. But it is possible to change your children's behaviour without criticizing them all the time.

Boosting self-confidence
Your children's self-confidence is vital to their psychological well-being. When their self-respect is strong, jealousy between them decreases. So boost their self-confidence whenever possible.

Developing co-operation
Although children are by nature sociable, they often have to be shown how to co-operate with each other, especially when they are young. Rivalry is stronger when children are unable to work together.

1. TREATING YOUR CHILDREN SERIOUSLY

Imagine how you would feel if everyone around you laughed whenever you made a comment that you wanted them to take seriously, or if your requests, complaints or questions were completely ignored. You would feel anxious, would start to harbour grudges and would become convinced that other people received better treatment than you. Well, your children are no different from you in this. If they feel that you regard them with shallow amusement rather than genuine respect, they will soon become jealous of each other. Here are some suggestions for encouraging your children to know that you take them seriously:

- *Listen to complaints.* The endless list of gripes and groans that your children have about each other can be irritating, and you may be tempted to dismiss them immediately. It is better to make time to listen to them – you will have to give them attention anyway if they start fighting one another.
- *Do not react with incredulity.* At times, some of your children's complaints about each other will probably seem ridiculous ('His bag of crisps had more in it than mine'). However, it is real enough to your child, so avoid giving a negative reaction as your first response.
- *Resist the guilt trap.* There is absolutely no point in making your child feel guilty because she is jealous of her sibling. She is not doing this deliberately, so you will gain nothing by berating her with comments like 'I'm shocked you're being so jealous. You are really terrible for saying that.'
- *Ask for reasons.* Always encourage your child to justify her complaints about her siblings, to offer an explanation for her comments. Ask her to provide hard evidence for her assertions rather than allowing her to make a general

moan about her brother or sister without justification

- *Offer explanations.* Make time to give reasons to your children when they have questioned a particular situation. For instance, explain to your older child that the reason why she has to set out the cutlery for the evening meal is because her younger brother did this task yesterday.

- *Emphasize the age gap.* Like it or not, your youngest child must face the fact that the others in the family are older and are therefore entitled to do some things that she cannot, such as going to bed later than her or being given more individual responsibility at home. Point out the age difference to her.

- *Be prepared for change.* None of us likes to think we are in the wrong, whether child or adult. But when one of your children complains that you are not treating her fairly, consider the possibility that she is right – you may unwittingly have created jealousy, and this needs to be altered.

- *Take action if necessary.* Having reached the conclusion that one of your children is unfairly advantaged compared to the others, take action to restore the balance. You need to follow your child's complaint through, assuming you agree it is correct.

- *Acknowledge her feelings.* Sometimes when your child approaches you about a perceived injustice, it is not really about that at all. Try to let her see that you know what her complaint is really about, for example, 'The real reason you are upset is because you did not do as well in your maths test as you wanted, isn't it?'

- *Verify that progress has been made.* When a complaint of unfairness has been raised with you, and you have responded either by an explanation or by taking action, do not leave it there. A few days later talk to your child in order to establish how she is feeling about it all now.

2. AVOIDING COMPARISONS

The horrible thing about comparisons is that there is always at least one loser. Clearly, the child who has the unfavourable standard will be unhappy that she is being shown up in a bad light when compared to her brother or sister. And even the child who has the desirable standard may not particularly enjoy her achievement being used in this way. In other words, in reality nobody wins. Comparisons of child against child — however well-intentioned — only intensify sibling rivalry, not reduce it. Here are some suggestions for avoiding the use of sibling comparisons in your family:

- *Treat each child individually.* Naturally you want each of your children to be as successful, as talented and as pleasant as the others. But you cannot make them be like that, despite all your efforts. Accept that your children are individuals with their own distinctive personality and characteristics.
- *Do not say it, even though you think it.* Having accepted in principle that comparisons are destructive and cause jealousy, you may still be tempted to make them, perhaps in a moment of peak frustration. While you cannot help thinking this, you should stop yourself from putting your thoughts into words.
- *Point out your concerns.* In most instances you will be able to express your concern without using another child in the family as a yardstick — for example, instead of saying, 'Your younger brother is able to keep his room tidy,' you could simply say 'Could you try to keep your room tidier?'
- *Focus on the positives.* Instead of comparing the negative aspects of one child against the positive aspects of another, take a more positive approach. For instance, 'Your hair looks nice today' is better than 'Why can't you dress smartly like your sister?'

- *Use differences constructively.* The fact that your children are all different is nothing to be afraid of, and can be constructive. You could, for example, ask your older child to use her more advanced learning skills to help the younger ones with a difficult number problem.
- *Encourage different leisure activities.* Just because your oldest child went to ballet classes and piano lessons does not mean your other children should follow suit. Let each child develop her own interests, even though this may not be as convenient as having all your children at the one activity.
- *Discourage others from making comparisons.* Other people who know your children may make comparisons between them, no matter what you do at home. If you find this happens, tactfully explain to the people concerned that you would rather each of your children were treated individually.
- *Speak to your children's teachers.* The chances are your children will be compared to each other when they are at school. This is extremely common. If this arises during your discussions at parents' night, explain your worry about comparisons to the teachers concerned.
- *Respond to self-generated comparisons.* One of your children may compare herself to her siblings, although you have never suggested this. Try to discourage her from making these self-generated comparisons by suggesting she concentrates on herself, not others.
- *Acknowledge achievements.* It is possible – and highly desirable – to praise one child's achievements or successes without reflecting this against the performance of the others. This helps all your children realize that they are each valued for their individual talents.

3. FAIRNESS, NOT EQUALITY

Like most parents, you probably make a conscientious effort to be fair to your children, so that each child gets her rightful share. Of course this is not always possible but is a goal worth aiming for – and there will be times when one of your children is absolutely convinced she is disadvantaged even though you can see nothing to justify this feeling. It is easy, however, to confuse fairness (that is, all your children getting what they need) with equality (each of your children getting exactly the same as the others), but this is unsatisfactory and will result in rivalry. Here are some suggestions to help you achieve fairness among your children:

- *Remember that equality means dissatisfaction.* Although your child moans and groans when she sees what you give her sibling, this does not mean she wants you to give her the same (even though that is what she says). Your child would probably be annoyed with you if you did!
- *Recognize individual needs.* Each child expresses her individual psychological needs in a distinctive way. For instance, one of your children might not be able to go to bed at night without a cuddle from you, whereas another may be content with a brief 'goodnight.'
- *Respond to these different needs.* It is often easier and more convenient when all your children need the same item, or want to attend the same activity. However, do not force them into this situation. In the long run it is better to meet their individual needs, according to each child's preference.
- *Do not worry about giving equal amounts.* The concept of 'equal amounts' is perceived differently by each of your children. Even if you give each of your children, for example, the same number of sweets, you may well find

that the older one complains she should get more because she is bigger.

- *Redress imbalances.* If one of your children does complain that she is not being treated fairly, then let her explain why she feels this way. She may be justified – and if she is, do whatever needs to be done to redress the situation so that she feels more comfortable about it.

- *Remind your children that you love them all.* Say it to them, regularly. Young children need this sort of reassurance – it is always comforting to hear mum and dad say how much they care. This helps reduce potential fears that you love one child more than the others.

- *Try not to have a favourite.* Some parents do find that they are particularly attached to one of the children, perhaps because she had a difficult birth or because she has such an endearing personality. If you do feel this way about one of your children, hide your feelings.

- *Make sure your oldest does not always get things before the others.* It is tempting to make your older child first for everything. After all, you reason to yourself, she is the oldest child in the family and she deserves to be first. But your younger children will resent this.

- *Spend money on your youngest sometimes.* Of course, buying new clothes for your oldest child is cost-effective, especially if she has younger sisters who can wear 'hand-me-downs'. But the youngest child also likes to have new clothes now and again.

- *Involve them in making decisions.* There will be plenty of occasions (such as family outings) when a group consensus has to be reached about the choice of activity. Try to involve all your children in the discussion, so that they can all express their points of view.

4. CHANGE WITHOUT CRITICISM

There are few things more emotionally draining than having to listen to your children bickering constantly with each other. And your response will probably be to criticize them for their negative behaviour – that is only natural. The problem is that your criticism only makes matters worse by getting everyone in a bad mood. Of course you want to change the situation so that fights are less frequent, but it is possible to do this through positive feedback instead of negative criticism. There is always a place for criticism in family life – after all, nobody is perfect – yet too much of it can create tense relationships at home. Here are some suggestions for changing the way your children behave towards each other, while keeping criticism to a minimum:

- *Think about how you feel when you are criticized.* You do not have a warm feeling when someone tells you what is wrong with you. You take it personally, no matter how hard you try not to – and your children feel the same way when you criticize them for bickering with each other.
- *Recognize the difference between criticizing your children and criticizing their behaviour.* It is better to say to your children 'Fighting with each other is unpleasant' (criticizing their behaviour) than to say 'You're nasty when you fight' (criticizing your children).
- *Establish the facts before you start to criticize.* You may be more interested in venting your frustration at their fighting than you are at establishing the underlying reasons. But finding out the facts is more likely to make your children feel they are being treated fairly.
- *Describe your children's feelings.* They may not know why their fight started in the first place, even when you ask them. In this situation, say to them what you think they

53

are feeling, for example, 'You both must be really angry with each other to shout like this.'

- *Aim for a resolution.* The pressure of their arguments may be so strong that you would find it easier to send them into separate rooms, with a severe reprimand, than to attempt to help them resolve their disagreement. Aiming for a resolution, however, is better in the long term.

- *Admit to difficulties.* There will be times when you do not know how to sort out their bickering. Be prepared to admit that to them. They will respond positively when you say 'I want to help you sort things out between you but I'm not sure how to do this. Let's discuss this together.'

- *Point out the positive aspects.* Rather than criticize them for the negative aspects of their rivalry, highlight the positive aspects of their relationship. For instance, you could say 'It's a pity you are arguing with each other at the moment because you were getting on so well together this morning.'

- *Set attainable targets.* If sibling rivalry seems perpetual, despite all your efforts to decrease it, then set a small target. Explain to your children that you do not want them to bicker, say, at tonight's family meal – and offer an incentive (such as an extra ten minutes' television-watching) for achieving this target.

- *Give them the promised reward.* When they do manage to reach the target you have set, give them the reward you promised. This is not bribery – rather, it is simply giving positive reinforcement for good behaviour in order to encourage them to behave the same way again in the future.

- *Praise them when they do not fight.* As soon as peace breaks out at home, you probably slump exhausted into a chair, glad to have a moment's rest without children fighting. Yet this is the time when you should praise your children for behaving so well – they will benefit from your encouragement.

5. BOOSTING SELF-CONFIDENCE

Your child's self-confidence comes from a number of sources, especially from the way other people react to her. Doubtless you have had days when you come home feeling thoroughly miserable all because someone made an adverse comment about your ability to organize your workload, or because your best friend is now a successful entrepreneur while you cannot manage to get even a part-time job. Like you, your child's 'feel-good' factor is susceptible to outside pressures. And a child with low self-confidence has such a low opinion of herself that she has difficulty getting on with her brothers and sisters – making sibling rivalry even stronger. Here are some suggestions of ways to boost your child's confidence:

- *Tell her what you especially like about her.* She is dwelling on the negatives, on the things she thinks are wrong with her. But you can dwell on the positives; telling her how much you enjoy her company and how she has a good sense of humour may help shift her perspective.
- *Let her make decisions.* Ask her what present she thinks her younger brother would like for his birthday, or what she would like to wear in her hair when she goes out at the weekend. Decision-making like this makes her feel you value her opinion.
- *Have clear ideas about family rules.* If your children do not know what you expect from them from one day to the next they will become anxious and upset, they will have little confidence in you or themselves, and they will probably bicker much more than they do at present.

- *Use a balance of rewards and punishment when controlling your children.* The most effective form of discipline is one that uses punishments to discourage naughty behaviour, and praise to encourage more desirable behaviour. Try to balance your use of these techniques.
- *Do not constantly run your child down.* Living with irritable and moody children is not easy, particularly when they fight a lot. But try to avoid complaining at them all the time – or else you will feel miserable because you have been nagging, and they will feel the same way too.
- *Let your child achieve success.* Success is one of the best boosts to self-confidence. If she has had a run of failures, for example with school work, then help her with her homework so that she achieves success. Avoid challenges that you know she will not meet.
- *Have realistic expectations.* Value your child's talents and abilities for what they are, even though you perhaps wish that she were more clever or athletic. This also means having realistic expectations of her achievements so that she is encouraged, not made despondent.
- *Split new targets into small stages.* New tasks can seem insurmountable to your child, but you can help her by breaking them down into small stages. Talk her through the stages in sequence, and encourage her patiently until she completes each step.
- *Encourage her to keep trying.* She may become downhearted when the learning process does not go smoothly, or when she sees others making bigger gains than her. Support her by persuading her to persist in her efforts until she succeeds – parental encouragement is very important.
- *Praise her achievements.* Everything is so exciting with your first child (her first word, her first reading book, etc.), and some parents find that this excitement lessens with each subsequent child. But these events matter to each

child no matter how many older siblings she has – so make a fuss.

6. DEVELOPING CO-OPERATION

Getting on with others in the family is very important. A peaceful family atmosphere is so relaxing compared to the tension that is generated by children who constantly niggle at each other and who are unable to co-operate even at a very basic level (such as deciding who gets into the bathroom first in the morning). There are many social skills that they have to learn, and part of your task as a parent is to teach these skills to your children so that they all become better at getting on with other people. Ways of developing your children's ability to behave caringly towards each other are discussed more fully in Chapter 7, but here are some brief suggestions for you to consider:

- *Encourage your children to communicate their feelings.* Sibling squabbles often stem from the children's inability to use words to communicate their feelings and ideas – they use fists instead. Ask your children questions about how they are feeling.
- *Discuss issues as a family.* Provide a regular informal forum in which every member of the family – not just you – can express his or her thoughts. Perhaps the best arrangement for this is the family evening meal, when everyone sits down together, parents and children.
- *When having family discussions, give everyone equal status.* It goes without saying that parents make the final decision on the big issues, but that still leaves room for everyone to have a say, and to be listened to while expressing a point of view.

- *Provide opportunities for sharing.* Many sibling fights start because one or more of the children are unable to share their toys. They will learn how to do this with practice, however, so do not make all the decisions about sharing for them – for example, ask one of them to share out a bag of sweets, and see how she gets on.
- *Show them how to co-operate, if necessary.* Give them a small household chore that requires co-operation (such as putting out cutlery on the table). If they begin to fight over who should do what, explain that one child can put out the knives, another the forks, and so on.
- *Play games with your children.* Your involvement allows you to assess their ability to take turns without becoming upset, and this is essential if they are ever to play together peacefully, without fighting. If one of your children becomes irritable because she is impatient for her turn, calm her.
- *Emphasize the importance of following rules.* To get on well with each other, your children need to be able to follow rules. One of them, however, might think this applies to everyone but her, so be prepared to remind her that rules matter and that this includes her as well.
- *Give limited responsibility for caring.* Although you should not saddle the older child with the responsibility of having to look after her younger brother all the time, there is no harm in asking her to do this occasionally. This enhances their relationship.
- *Provide a good model yourself.* Children who see their parents snapping at each other regularly will soon come to regard this as a normal way of life, and they will start to behave in the same way towards each other. You do not need to be a saint, but do not let your children see you and your partner bickering constantly.
- *Praise co-operation.* Give your children lots of praise when you see spontaneous examples of co-operation, for

example when they help each other tidy toys away. Your attention and pleasure at these incidents will increase the likelihood of their being repeated.

SUMMARY

You cannot avoid sibling rivalry altogether, but you can control it. Do not leave your children's relationships to chance. There is a lot you can do at home to minimize the level of sibling rivalry in your family: treat your children with respect, avoid comparisons between brothers and sisters, strive for fairness rather than equality, try not to use criticism too often, boost your children's self-confidence and develop their co-operation.

5

· · · · ·

How to Stop their Fights

THE FACTS

Aggression is common in young children, including yours.
And you need not think it only happens in your family — here
are some facts about fighting during the pre-school years that
have been revealed by extensive psychological surveys of families:

- The peak age for fighting among brothers and sisters is
  when the youngest child reaches the age of about 4. At
  this age he wants to play co-operatively with his siblings
  and so he spends more time in their company — hence
  there are more opportunities for disagreements among
  them.
- When your child is 2 or 3 years old he prefers to
  express his anger and aggression using his fists. Most
  young children are very quick to raise their hands against
  their siblings when they get annoyed with them, even
  though the siblings may be years older.
- Most of the fights that your toddler has with his older or
  younger siblings start over something very practical, such
  as a game or a cuddly toy. Think about the last fight
  your children had — almost certainly it began when they
  both wanted to play with the same toy at the same time.
- By the time your child is 4 or 5, the focus of his

aggression has changed. In most instances he does not just want to achieve a practical result – he wants to cause distress to the sibling who has annoyed him. That is why he is actually pleased when his brother or sister bursts into tears after a fight; he has achieved his goal.

- Children vary in their level of aggressiveness and in their willingness to fight with others. You may have a child who lets his siblings walk all over him, without complaining at all, while another of your children might start a fight over something very trivial. Much depends on your child's personality.

Frightening, isn't it, to think that there is so much hostility at this early stage in a child's life? Yet society – and perhaps you as a parent – can give out conflicting messages to young children about the value placed on aggressiveness. You will have lost count of the number of children's television programmes with a violent content – the fact that the violence appears to be benign, often in cartoon form, does not stop it from being violence all the same. There is aggression in films as well, where the struggling underdog literally fights his way to the top. And aggression is valued in sport; you have probably found yourself encouraging your children to try hard at a particular activity, to push themselves as far as possible in order to achieve. Maybe you have even encouraged them to stand up for themselves in nursery or school when another child tries to take advantage of them.

The message your child receives from these sources is that aggression is valued and that fighting with others is an acceptable way to achieve goals. The difficulty facing him, however, is knowing when this rules applies and when it does not. Your young child has not yet realized the difference between aggressiveness that you are likely to praise and aggressiveness you will chastise him for. He needs your guidance on the management of his aggression.

WHERE DOES IT COME FROM?

Psychologists studying the level of fighting between siblings tend to disagree about the source of aggressive behaviour. There are several common explanations:

1. Innate Influences on Aggression

Some psychologists claim that aggression is innate, that a baby arrives in this world already pre-programmed with the capacity to be angry and hostile. And when you look at a new baby screaming angrily in his cot because he is hungry and wants more food, then you may agree with this perspective! Proponents of this theory argue that, since there is little doubt that children do have innate needs (such as the need to eat, the need to drink and the need to be loved), it stands to reason that other needs could also be innate (such as the need to be aggressive and the need to fight for self-protection). This may not seem a very attractive view of early development, but it could account for the high level of aggression in young children.

The main difficulty with this explanation, however, is that there is no hard evidence to support it, while there is plenty of evidence which challenges it. For instance, there are many children who appear to have no innate aggressiveness whatsoever, who let other children physically attack them rather than defend themselves. For these children, aggression is not second nature – if anything, it goes completely against their natural impulses.

2. Social Influences on Aggression

Another explanation for the incidence of aggression in young children is that it depends on the extent to which hostility and fighting are accepted within society. In a society where aggression is highly valued, members of that society are rewarded for their aggression. And there are plenty of examples throughout history to support this argument. In countries with oppressive and violent regimes, the level of street violence – from people not directly connected with the regime – tends to be higher. It is as though tolerance of violence at a broad level within society encourages more violence at an individual level, because it creates an atmosphere in which fighting between people is normal.

While this may be true, it can hardly be maintained with any credibility that a pre-school child bickers more with his siblings because the society in which he lives takes a tolerant view of hostility. Young children simply are not aware of social ideals, and are therefore not influenced by them. In addition, aggression in young children seems to be a universal phenomenon found in every culture, irrespective of the laws of the land.

3. Television's Influence on Aggression

Considerable attention has been paid to the influence of television on the malleable minds of developing young children. There are several reasons for this, for example statistics confirm that pre-school children spend a substantial number of hours every day watching television (often unsupervised), there are many young children who watch television late in the evening when the programmes are more suited to adult tastes, and the level of violence portrayed (often quite explicitly) in the media is much higher than ever before. Although there is no convincing experimental evidence that children are influenced by what they see on television, common sense tells you that there has to be a connection.

You need only watch a group of 4- or 5-year-olds after they have watched a programme featuring their favourite martial arts hero – in their play scenarios they will start acting out some of what they have just seen on the television. This suggests that there could be a strong link between the two. However, much as though you might want to ban your child from watching these programmes, this strategy does not offer a long-term solution (because he will hear about them from his friends, or might even be able to watch them when he visits his friends' houses.)

A more effective strategy is to talk to your child about the programme while he watches it, and again after the programme has finished. A young child often has difficulty distinguishing fact from fantasy, and he may believe that people can get kicked and punched without being hurt because that is what he sees on television. The danger is that he construes the fantasy as reality. So remind him that what he sees on television is not real, that the people shown on-screen are only pretending. Tell him explicitly that when children get punched, kicked or beaten in real life, it really does hurt and it really does make them cry. This seems terribly obvious to you, but it probably is not so clear to your child. Spell it out to him – even if he does not grasp what you say the first time, your message will sink in eventually.

4. Parental Influence

There is no doubt that the greatest influence on the expression and development of aggression in your children is the way you raise them. Numerous studies have investigated the effects of different styles of parenting, and have proved that the way you maintain discipline at home is directly linked to the frequency of fighting between your children at home. (This is discussed fully in Chapter 7.)

Psychological research has shown that there are two other major parental influences on a child's aggression. First, their own use of violence and hostility. Where parents use physical punishment when they see their children fighting with each other, the chances are that this actually increases the children's aggression and the level of sibling rivalry. The reason for this is straightforward: Your children copy you. If you use violence to sort out your problems then they will as well. You may be tempted to smack your children when they repeatedly fight with each other, but you can hardly expect them to behave differently from the way you do.

The second parental influence (apart from discipline) is the speed at which you respond to your children's aggressiveness. In many instances parents do not interfere when their children first start to fight. Perhaps you are busy with another task and do not want to be distracted. Or maybe you would prefer that your children learn to sort out disputes between themselves without your input. Once tempers become very heated and fists start to fly, then you step in angrily. Unfortunately, this creates confusion in your children's minds because you have allowed a limited amount of fighting – and they have no idea of the extent of that limit. In a sense, you have partly rewarded their fighting by ignoring it, and they may assume that a limited physical conflict is permissible the next time.

HOW TO REDUCE YOUR CHILDREN'S AGGRESSION

Here are some suggestions for minimizing aggression and fighting between your children:

- *Avoid extremes when controlling your children*. Even though you may be extremely disappointed and upset when you discover your children hitting each other, do not over-react. Keep calm and be reasonable. Let them see that you are angry with them but that you still love them.
- *Aim for self-discipline, not blind obedience*. Help your children develop into well-balanced individuals who can

cope with the stresses and strains of everyday life. A warm, caring relationship between you and your children reduces their aggression towards each other.

- *Do not argue with your partner about discipline in front of your children.* Talk about family discipline in private, away from the ears of your curious young children. When children perceive ambiguity in their parents' rules and expectations, they may take this as a licence for aggressiveness.

- *Use words, not smacking, as a punishment for aggression.* Give your child a verbal reprimand – not a thump – in response to his aggression towards his siblings. It is more effective than smacking because he does not like being told off by you in front of his brothers and/or sisters.

- *Talk to your children.* Even at the age of 3 or 4 years, a child is old enough to understand an explanation that takes the feelings of others into consideration. You will find that your children appreciate your arguments against aggression when you encourage them to think of other people's feelings.

- *If they do watch a lot of television, supervise their viewing.* They may want to watch the same type of action programme night after night. Do not let them. Instead, make sure that they watch other programmes which have a non-violent content.

- *Tell them why aggression is so unpleasant.* Make it quite clear – for example, 'When you hit your sister on the arm it hurts her and makes her cry. It also makes me very angry with you.' Your young child might not realize the practical effect of his violence, so it is worth pointing it out to him.

- *Do not coerce your children into co-operating.* You are bigger than your children, and if you scream at them loudly enough they will do whatever you say – at least for the time being. However, once your yelling stops and they

are out of your sight, their fighting will start all over
again.
* *Allow your children to have aggressive feelings.* Most children
do feel angry and hostile towards their siblings
sometimes, and there is little you can do about it. You
can insist, however, that they do not turn these aggressive feelings into physically aggressive behaviour.

THE NEED FOR ATTENTION

Every child loves attention from mum and dad – and he is
usually prepared to do anything in order to get it. This means
that your children's squabbling could be attention-seeking
behaviour – in other words, it could have the sole purpose
of making sure you take notice of them. The chart below lists
some reasons why bickering between your children might be
motivated in this way.

Reason	Explanation
Learning	If you get involved with your children every single time they start fighting with each other, they will soon learn that this is a very effective way to grab your attention. They may start to fight with each other deliberately just to achieve this aim, and so the battles will continue despite your efforts to stop them.
Reward	Although you might think your reprimand and punishment will discourage your children from fighting in the future, it might have the opposite effect. They would probably prefer that you shouted at them rather than ignored them. In this way, your

	attention becomes a reward, not a punishment.
Solution	Your children may have realized that when they have a disagreement with each other they are rarely able to resolve it themselves. However, they may also have discovered that your intervention is successful because you always sort the fight out for them – hence they deliberately argue within your hearing.
Making Up	Once the fight is over and you have chastised them for their misbehaviour, there will be a point where you all make up with each other and become friends again. They will probably enjoy this stage because it brings them close to you again – this might make all the unpleasantness worthwhile for them.

Controlling Attention

Keeping these points in mind, consider the following techniques for dealing effectively with your children when you think that their fighting is simply attention-seeking behaviour:

- *Show interest in them when they are not bickering.* Teach them that they do not need to fight with each other for you to spend time with them. Do this by making sure you always have some time each day to play with your children or to take them on a short outing. True, you probably have a busy schedule, rushing from here to there, often so that your children can get to their activities in plenty of time. But they still need to have time with you. Be philosophical – they will get your attention anyway by misbehaving, so you may as well spend time with them when they are not fighting.

68

- *Do not get involved immediately.* Some parents have a very low tolerance of bickering between their children and intercede the moment tension first arises. While this reaction is understandable, it takes the responsibility for resolving disputes away from the children and places it squarely with you. All the children have to do is start the fight, because they know you will stop it for them. If possible, hang back for a few moments before reacting. You might be pleasantly surprised to discover that your children are able to sort things out without using violence against each other.

- *Do not give your attention to the child who is acting aggressively.* When you see your children fighting, you will probably react by giving the aggressor your attention ('Stop hitting your sister. Come with me into the other room so she can have some peace'). This rewards the child's misbehaviour with your attention and he may do the same again in the future. Instead, look after the child who has been on the receiving end of the aggression ('Come with me, and I'll wipe your tears away'), so that she is the one who gets all your attention.

TEN-POINT ACTION PLAN FOR RESOLVING CONFLICTS PEACEFULLY

Even though you follow all the suggestions given earlier in this chapter, there will be times when your children are locked together in a siblings' dispute. Here is a Ten-Point Action Plan for dealing with these fights:

1. *Try to ignore them.* Of course you have to take action when your children are at each other's throats, or when they are clearly upset. But try not to get involved when

69

they are routinely bickering – ignoring them may end their minor argument more quickly than rewarding them with your attention.

2. *Do not drag them apart, then put them into separate rooms.* Unless absolutely necessary, keep them together when trying to resolve their disagreement. This is the only way they can learn from their experience; separation just keeps their anger simmering.

3. *Be objective.* Avoid the temptation to blame one child in particular. For instance, saying 'Why are you slapping your little brother?' increases ill-feeling, whereas saying 'I can see that you're both really angry with each other' is a more neutral statement.

4. *Confirm the rules.* Explain to them that while they have a right to disagree with each other – because at this stage you do not know the cause – they do not have a right to raise their hands to each other. Make sure they know that this particular rule applies no matter what the provocation is.

5. *Calm them, then listen.* Your next step should be to calm them down, using a relaxed, steady voice – not screaming in rage at them. Ask each child to sit on a separate chair and then ask them one at time to give their own account of the circumstances leading up to the fight.

6. *Restate the problem.* Children often have difficulty thinking clearly when they are upset. So summarize the disagreement for them, for example, 'The problem appears to be that you both want to watch a different television programme at the same time, and you can't decide who should choose.'

7. *Ask them to develop a solution.* It is their problem, so ask them to think of ways that the argument can be resolved. Encourage your children to look at all sides of the issue, taking everyone's perspective into account before making a suggestion. Emphasize the need for compromise.

8. *If they cannot reach a solution themselves, suggest one.* Ideally your children should achieve a resolution themselves, but be prepared to make suggestions if they cannot, such as 'You could both watch one programme today and then both watch the other tomorrow.' Persist until agreement is reached.
9. *Carry out the agreed solution.* Supervise the children – if necessary – so that they stick to the agreement. You may have to remind them of their specific agreement and how they agreed it should be carried out. Your involvement ensures fairness.
10. *Praise them for resolving their conflict.* Show them how pleased you are that they managed to resolve their dispute without lashing out at each other. And do this even when you have to 'police' the arrangements. In time they will get used to this form of non-violent conflict resolution.

SUMMARY

Aggression is common in children, although psychologists tend to disagree about its origin. Popular explanations are that it is innate, that it is influenced by society, that it is influenced by television and that it is influenced by parents. Whatever the real explanation, there are many things you can do to reduce the level of your children's aggression.

Sometimes children fight simply in order to gain their parents' attention. If you show interest in your children only when they fight with each other, they will soon learn to instigate fights just to gain your attention. However, some fights are inevitable. When they do occur, get actively involved to show your children how they can resolve conflicts peacefully, without resorting to violence.

6
. . . . .

Violence in Families

DIFFERENT STANDARDS

Families can be violent. Verbal and physical violence between children and adults are used routinely in some families as part of their everyday interactions. We all know of parents who seem to be unusually hostile towards their children when they misbehave, and whose children seem to scream at each other for the slightest thing. Yet the general level of violence within a family affects the way siblings relate to each other; violent parents have violent children.

One landmark survey of several thousand nationally-representative 'typical' families considered the level of violence at home. 'Violence' was the term used to describe acts that included throwing something at another person, grabbing her hard, shoving her aggressively, slapping, kicking, biting or punching another person, hitting her with a solid object, beating her up and threatening to use a weapon against her. The results of the survey revealed that:

- In over 15 per cent of the families, parents used violence against each other.
- In over 60 per cent of the families, parents used violence against their children.
- In over 15 per cent of the families, children used violence against their parents.

- In over 75 per cent of the families, children used violence against each other.

These figures confirm that in everyday life families can be violent environments in which to live. Although few parents openly condone violence between their children, equally few parents would regard sibling aggression as abnormal. Most people accept a basic level of antagonism between their children; this acceptance increases the likelihood of physical violence between siblings. That is why it is important for you to think about the standards you have at home, the limits of aggressive behaviour which you regard as acceptable, and the model of behaviour you and your partner present to your children.

BULLYING IN THE FAMILY

The stark truth is that bullying is not confined to schools – it is a frightening reality for many brothers and sisters who have to cope with the torments of a sibling who bullies them almost every day of their lives. True, many young children become wild when playing together at home, but this is not bullying, because malicious intent is lacking – a deliberate nastiness towards siblings is one of the hallmarks of the genuine domestic bully.

Bullying can take many forms. For instance, it can involve the **use of language** (that is, the bully may use threats, teasing or insults against her younger brother); it can involve the **use of the body** (the bully may make rude gestures with her hands, or may kick, trip or slap her sibling); and/or it can be **psychological** (the bully may use a menacing facial expression or may hint that she is scheming against her sibling).

In many instances the **act of bullying may seem**

73

innocuous to an onlooker because it appears to be part of the normal sibling relationship (such as when a child teases her sibling because he is not very good at football). But the constant repetition of these apparently benign remarks wears down the victim. The impact of the taunts adds up over time, and the sibling on the receiving end starts to dread the next one. **The effect builds up**, it does not attenuate.

Every type of bullying involves an **abuse of power**. To you, the thought of your 4-year-old being powerful might seem ridiculous. But when she grabs a toy off her younger sister and then glances at her menacingly to keep her from complaining about it, it is her relative power that enables her to be so manipulative and controlling. Perhaps your timid 2-year-old has been told by you to do as her older sibling says. Your 4-year-old may interpret this as licence to do as she likes regarding her younger sister.

Looked at this way, many of the typical acts of aggression between siblings – especially when the balance of power constantly lies in favour of the older and stronger child, although it can be vice versa – are forms of bullying, and therefore bullying is more common at home than most parents like to think. Bullying may not be obvious to mum and dad. Your child might withstand bullying from her sibling for months and months without saying anything to you, for fear of retribution.

Why Children Bully

There is no single reason to account for bullying in a family. Each of the psychological influences outlined in the chart below might play a part in determining the bully's aggressive reactions towards others. If you have a child who bullies her siblings, consider all of these possibilities.

Reason	Explanation
Imitation	Most of your child's behaviour is learned – and

one of the most important ways she learns is by imitating you. This process occurs naturally. This is why bullying parents tend to have children who try to bully one another.

Anger
Every child gets angry sometimes; she needs to be able to express that anger non-violently. However, if she is reprimanded by mum and dad every time she complains about something, she will release her anger by bullying her weaker siblings.

Sadness
There are many potential causes of sadness in childhood, such as resentment of siblings, rejection by friends and lack of success in school. Any of these factors – if they are severe and long-lasting – can cause a child to bully her siblings.

Abuse
A child who is physically or sexually abused will be frightened and will have difficulty trusting others. As a result she may not be able to sustain good sibling relationships, and this may be expressed in the form of bullying her siblings.

Pressure
Every child wants to achieve in all that she does. But when a child is pressurized by her parents to succeed – especially when she is not capable of achieving their high standard – her disappointment may turn into a desire to bully her brother or sister.

SIBLING COMBINATIONS

Studies have investigated the means by which children coerce their siblings to do what they want, and how these means vary depending on the particular sibling combination (older brother with younger sister, younger brother with older sister). The results show that aggression is found in almost every combination, but the following distinctive effects also emerged:

Type of Bullying	Sibling Combination
Physical assaults	two sisters; boy with an older brother
Verbal assaults	two brothers; two sisters
Use of anger and fear	two sisters; boy with an older brother

Acts of bullying are least likely to occur in families with an older boy and a younger girl.

THE VICTIM

However, the situation is not entirely one-sided. If one of your children complains that she is being bullied by one of her siblings, take time to consider both sides. Research indicates that there are several types of victims of bullying in addition to the **genuine victim** who has done nothing to incur the wrath of her siblings and who has tried to stop the bullying before asking you for support.

A child who is a **weak victim** does not have the aggression needed to stand up for herself when confronted by a hostile sibling; nor does she have strong enough relationships with her other siblings to call on them for support when she is bullied. She gets picked on because she cannot defend herself effectively, because none of the other children in the family is prepared to stand up for her, and because she cries pathetically when provoked. Simply put, she is an easy target because of her low resistance.

On the other hand, the child who is a **deliberate victim**

quite intentionally provokes her siblings into assaulting her; for instance she may taunt her older brother or sister even though she knows what the consequences will be, or she might tear one of her brother's favourite books in the full knowledge that he will probably lash out at her when he finds out. She does this because she has an unconscious need to be noticed by her siblings.

Then there is the **willing victim**, who lets herself be picked on because it is a useful and effective way of getting sympathy – her parents fuss all over her when she reports her siblings' behaviour to them.

When listening to claims about bullying from one of your children, check that she is not a **make-believe victim** – in other words, make sure that she really is being bullied. Like the willing victim, a make-believe victim has also learned that claims of maltreatment at the hands of her brothers or sister earn her parental sympathy and concern. She is prepared to make up one story after another until you listen to her.

When you discover instances of sibling bullying, think about the role of the victim as well. This will help you to clarify the real cause of the antagonism between your children and what you can do to help them reduce the violence in their relationship.

WHAT TO DO

If one of your children complains that she is being bullied by her sibling – and if you are satisfied that these claims are genuine – then you can help her in the following ways:

- *Never make light of her complaints.* It is a serious matter to her and she needs you to respond positively. The chances are that she will be upset when telling you about her sibling's behaviour. Always reassure her that you will not do anything without talking to her first.

- *Suggest that she keeps out of her sibling's way in the mean time.* For example, she could go to another room when her brother or sister starts to pick on her; or she can try to avoid them when they appear to be in a bad mood. There is no point in looking for trouble.

- *Persuade her to keep a neutral expression on her face when she is being bullied.* The sibling who bullies wants her to be afraid, because it meets his or her emotional need to be powerful. If the victim can remain calm, without crying or becoming upset, the bullying may settle down.

- *Never encourage retaliation.* It is up to you to stop your child from bullying – it is not a job for your other children. First, your children are different ages, so a younger child's attempts at retaliation could backfire. As well as this, you would simply be encouraging more violence at home.

- *Reassure her that it is perfectly acceptable to ask you for help.* She may need to be convinced that she is not being a sneak by approaching you – children often have a very black-and-white attitude towards issues like this. Tell her you want her to let you know about any further incidents.

- *Be seen to take action.* What you do in response to hearing that one of your children is bullying a sibling will determine the course of the bullying in future. If you are seen to do very little or nothing at all, then it will continue. If you try to stop it, then sibling bullying is less likely to occur again.

TACKLING THE BULLY

As well as helping the victim cope, you also need to tackle the bully herself, even though this can be very difficult for you to do. Admitting to yourself that you have a child who is bullying is not easy. Yet it has to be done.

Always act quickly when you think bullying has occurred within your family. Hear all sides of the story, consider whether or not bullying really has taken place, then speak to the child who has been doing the bullying. But do not do this in an angry manner, and do not do it in front of your other children – the embarrassment that this would cause the bully will only lead to an escalation of the situation. Instead, take the child into another room, sit her down facing you, and explain how you see things. Most children will respond positively when they feel that they are being spoken to by their parent in a non-threatening way. Listen to her side of the story, all the time emphasizing the need to think of her brothers and sisters and the effect that her behaviour has on them.

Explain to your child who has been bullying that her actions are not acceptable, spelling out clearly the implications of what she has done. After all, she may not have realized the full impact of her behaviour. Talk to her about how she would feel if the roles were reversed, if she were the victim. Make sure that any punishments are non-physical, such as sending her to bed early, depriving her of an outing that weekend, not letting her play with her friends for a day, and so on. And advise her of the consequences of any similar actions in the future. Tell the child who has been bullied about the action you have taken.

SUMMARY

Families vary in the level of violence tolerated, but aggression is often used routinely. In some instances a child bullies her siblings as a means of controlling them. Bullying can be verbal as well as physical, and there are many different reasons why a child feels the needs to bully her brothers and sisters, including failure, sadness and pressure. The sibling combination with the lowest level of physical or verbal tension is when there is a girl with an older brother.

In some instances a child may intentionally become a victim of sibling aggression, and you should consider this possibility. However, never trivialize complaints of bullying, and always help your child (the victim) deal with the situation. Of course, you must also help your other child (the bully) to find more positive ways of relating to her siblings. Never punish a bully physically.

7

· · · · ·

Family Discipline:
When It Begins

THE IMPORTANCE OF DISCIPLINE

The style of discipline you have at home affects the level of
bickering between your children. For example, when there is
no firm discipline there is likely to be more fighting among
the siblings because the children are allowed to act on their
first impulse instead of reflecting before taking action. Or, if
there is a very repressive discipline at home the children may
niggle at each other because they are not allowed to express
their feelings in any other way. This does not mean that discipline is automatically destructive and limiting, a way of
making children compliant to adult wishes. Discipline helps
your children get on well together.

Five Benefits of Discipline

Here are some sound psychological reasons why discipline
benefits your child:

1. *Confidence.* A good standard of discipline at home makes
   your children feel at ease, confident in their relationships
   with each other. This happens because they know what
   to expect from their siblings and they know what their
   siblings expect of them. Since your children follow the
   family rules most of the time, they have a sense of trust

in one another; this makes them feel more at ease when they are together.

2. *Framework*. Human nature is such that children need some structure in their day-to-day existence. They need to have some certainty about what comes next, otherwise they become confused and anxious. Of course they like variety and excitement, but they need to have basic consistency in their lives so that they can cope with change. A well-established discipline at home fulfils this psychological need.

3. *Caring*. One of the side-effects of sound family discipline is that your children are encouraged to think about the feelings of others. Rules focus your children's attention on their own behaviour and makes them think about this in relation to your expectations of them. They realize that their actions affect you – and others in the family – and this stops them from thinking only of themselves and their own needs all the time.

4. *Limits*. Most psychologists would agree that children like to explore as far as they can; like all explorers, they prefer to test uncharted territory. That is why your toddler, for instance, empties milk onto the floor even though you specifically told him not to. Without limits on behaviour at home, your children would not know when to stop. Discipline sets these limits for your children – they know that there is a line that is not to be crossed.

5. *Popularity*. Your children have to know how to behave properly when you are not there to tell them what to do, such as when they are at a friend's house or at nursery or school. A strong and identifiable discipline at home provides your children with a system of behaviour that they can apply independently to themselves wherever they are. So discipline means that other people will enjoy their company, too.

DISCIPLINING YOUR BABY

Like all parents, you have to decide when to start introducing discipline into your child's life. Some people will tell you that you have to start laying down rules and regulations as soon as your baby arrives, and that you should establish a routine with him as soon as possible. Others will tell you that there is plenty of time to develop discipline and that you should just enjoy your baby's company. You have to make up your own mind on this issue. However, many popular ideas about discipline with young babies have no evidence to support them.

Popular Idea

You should not pick up your crying baby too often, as that will put him in control of you, not vice-versa.

Why This Is Wrong

Your young baby's cry is a reflex reaction. Crying is his way of communicating with you; it is his way of telling you that he is hungry, upset or uncomfortable. He cannot express these feelings to you any other way. Of course, he may learn that if he cries long enough you are bound to come to him eventually, but he certainly will not have learned this in the first few days or weeks of life. Therefore, it does not make sense to ignore him when he is crying – all he is doing is asking you for help.

Popular Idea

Leaving your baby to cry sometimes teaches him that he cannot always get his own way; the process of discipline starts at this age.

Why This Is Wrong

Leaving a baby to cry teaches him that his mum and dad are not prepared to comfort him when he is upset. Remember

83

that he is totally dependent on you for everything at this stage in his life – he needs you to feed him, to keep him warm, to wash him when he is dirty and to change his nappy when it is soiled. If you do not meet these developmental needs he will feel lonely and miserable, which will make him cry even more.

Popular Idea

If you do not start exercising discipline with your baby you will have a difficult job dealing with him when he is older.

Why This Is Wrong

Discipline is a system of rules about the way a child should behave himself and about the way he should behave towards others. Put this way, the thought of a baby needing discipline seems absurd, since his understanding is not sufficiently developed to grasp these complex ideas. He cannot possibly think of other people until much later, when he is older. There is no established connection between rigid rules in the early months and behaviour in later childhood.

Popular Idea

A baby feels insecure and unloved without discipline; he feels as though nobody cares for him.

Why This Is Wrong

Your baby relies heavily on his senses in the first few months of life. He feels loved when he sees you close up, smiling at him and when he hears you speaking softly and gently to him. He feels loved when you hold him close in order to calm him during a bout of tears, and when you stroke his face gently as he falls asleep. These very basic responses are the actions that make him feel safe and cared for – discipline does not have this effect on a young baby.

Popular Idea

You must pick up your baby every time he cries because he might hurt himself and begin to resent you.

Why This Is Wrong

While you should not ignore your baby every time he cries, he will not come to any harm from being left on his own for a moment or two – this is quite different from always leaving him to cry unless he is due a feed. Sometimes, he will cry out of boredom. When that happens you may find that the crying stops before you become involved, as your baby has found something in his cot or pram to amuse himself. Pausing for a moment or two before going to him can increase his independence.

Probably the best approach to discipline when your baby is young is to take a reasonable and balanced approach when he cries. You do not need to rush anxiously to him the moment you hear him making a sound, nor should you pretend that you cannot hear him. Either extreme is unproductive; try to find the middle ground where you respond to his cries on most occasions but not every single time, where you sometimes wait a moment or two before attending to him. You will have to use your own judgement on this.

Now He's a Toddler

By the time your infant is around 1 year old, he begins to understand that you have clear ideas about his behaviour and that you are prepared to stop him from misbehaving. From now on, the process of establishing discipline begins in earnest. And by the time he is a toddler, challenging your family rules is his full-time business!

Toddlers are so full of their own importance – a child of this age begins to realize that he has an identity separate from his parents, that he has his own ideas and feelings. And, being at a developmental stage in which he is still sees the world only from his point of view, your toddler expects to get things his own way.

This period in a child's life has been nicknamed 'the terrible 2s', largely because your child's behaviour can be so unreasonably demanding. Most parents find this a stressful time. Many report that the constant battle of wills between themselves and their toddler is exhausting, as each becomes more and more determined to gain control over the other. Lots of these confrontations over discipline, however, can be avoided.

Consider 2-year-old Colin, who – like most young children his age – has an insatiable curiosity to know how things work. Almost every day he and his mum have a disagreement about the gas fire in their sitting room. She has warned him repeatedly to keep his hands away from the safety grill when the fire is on, yet rarely a day goes by without Colin trying to touch it – the prospect of burnt fingers does not deter this behaviour. Whenever his mum reprimands him for touching the safety grill, he just continues regardless. No matter how many times she tells him to stop, Colin keeps putting his fingers against it. Eventually she loses her temper with him and places him on the other side of the room away from the gas fire, but within a moment or two he makes his way back across the floor so that he can repeat the action his mum is so keen to discourage.

When Colin's mum finally realized that her toddler was ignoring her completely and doing what he wanted despite her intervention, she tried an alternative strategy. Instead of waiting until Colin began playing with the safety grill, she decided to distract his attention (using his favourite toy) as soon as he looked as though he was likely to make a move towards it. This proved successful. The pattern of constant confrontations was broken and Colin soon forgot about his habit of touching the safety grill.

This sort of strategy is not always possible, but it can be very effective in reducing battles over discipline. Managing your toddler is not simply about imposing control over him, otherwise you and he would be fighting with each other all day – and he would probably be aggressive towards his siblings too. A large part of discipline at this age involves helping your child avoid the potential pitfalls that lie in front of him.

PERSONALITY

Discipline varies from family to family, and even from child to child in some instances. Perhaps you have found that you need to be very firm with one of your children (because he never does what you tell him the first time) whereas you can be more lenient with his sister (because she rarely bends the rules). In other words, the way you develop discipline at home depends partly on your children. There are three main personality characteristics when it comes to responding to discipline:

1. *Adaptable.* A child who is adaptable has no problem adjusting to change. Rather than desperately clinging to what he is used to, this type of child likes to try out new experiences, new ideas and suggestions. He rarely complains. This means that when mum and dad set limits on behaviour, he adapts easily to their expectations. He does not challenge them.
2. *Resistant.* Totally different from the adaptable child, a child with this type of personality does not like routine. He is highly resistant to change, preferring to do what he wants. He is not very good at responding positively to other people's suggestions. Discipline, therefore, is very difficult with a resistant child because he does not

87

like rules that have been set by anyone other than himself.

3. *Passive.* A child who is passive does not have strong opinions about anything. So if he is given the same toys each day, for instance, he will play happily with them without complaining of boredom. Although passivity means he does not actively challenge the rules set down by his parents, it does mean that he often needs a lot of persuasion to do what is asked of him.

SUMMARY

Discipline is important for your children because it gives them confidence and provides a framework in their lives. Although there are different views regarding disciplining a young baby, there is little doubt that setting standards starts in earnest when your child becomes a toddler.

8

. . . . .

Different Types of Discipline

PARENT CHARACTERISTICS

The way you administer discipline with your children depends in part on your own characteristics. Parents tend to create a discipline which reflects their particular personality.

Talia is a very shy sort of person who does not enjoy meeting others. She expects children to be reasonably quiet when playing. Consequently, at home she sets rules in order to stop her children from being too noisy or boisterous. This form of discipline has a direct effect on their development. For example, both children are very timid, rarely take part in energetic play activities, and always look agitated whenever games become slightly raucous.

Compare this with Pauline, who is very outgoing. She encourages her son and daughter to have as much fun as they can, and her discipline at home is very flexible because of this – they are allowed a lot more freedom than most children of their age. And this shows in their behaviour – when playing, they join in every activity wholeheartedly.

This connection between your personality and views on discipline is normal. However, it can constrain your children. After all, what suits your personality may not suit your child's personality.

A similar effect is seen in upbringing. Your discipline is probably directly related to the way you were raised, even though you may be unaware of the link between your experiences as a child and your outlook in later life.

For instance, when a parent has strong feelings of resentment about the way she was raised during childhood, she may be determined that her own children will have an entirely different experience. That is why adults who grew up in a household where regular smacking was the norm – and who do not have happy memories of this – often totally reject the suggestion of physical punishment for their own children. On the other hand, someone who has very fond memories of childhood will try to recreate a similar atmosphere for her own children.

In this way you are influenced by your past, by the events that took place at home during your own formative years. That is inevitable. Yet it is important to pause for a moment to consider the reasons underlying your choice of discipline, and in particular to consider whether the discipline you administer is actually in the best interests of your children, or whether it is simply a pattern that you have fallen into without thinking about it too deeply.

Single Parents

Establishing discipline as a single parent can be more difficult than as a partner in a two-parent family, yet it is just as important for the children. It is also important for the single parent, who wants family life to be free of sibling rivalry.

There is a greater potential for sibling rivalry in single-parent families for the reasons listed in the chart below:

Reason	Explanation
Attention	Children vie for their parents' attention in a two-parent family at the best of times, each child wanting a share of mum's and dad's time. When only one parent is around competition

for his or her attention is greater. Tension and rivalry between siblings are more likely in these circumstances.

Tiredness
A single parent has to carry out the work that is normally shared by two parents, and this can be exhausting. She probably has to hold down a job, ferry the children all over the place and make sure the house runs like clockwork. Amid all of these pressures, she has to find time to talk to each child individually – and she may be too tired at the end of the day to do this.

Confidence
As a single parent, she has to make all the decisions about child-related matters, and probably has to do this by herself, without discussing it with anyone. As a result she may not be fully confident in her ability to make correct decisions. If her children sense her lack of self-confidence, they are more likely to bicker in order to try to change her mind.

Resentment
The single-parent family may have arisen from the separation or divorce of the parents. So the children could harbour unresolved feelings of resentment and anger for what has happened, directed at both parents. This negative feeling could well be expressed through general niggling and occasional fighting between the children.

Challenges
In a two-parent family, there are usually two adults to set standards of behaviour and to make sure these standards are kept by the children. When there is only one parent to implement discipline, the children are more likely to be challenging and argumentative (one parent is easier to tackle than two), and this may spill over into their sibling relationships.

Despite these predispositions for sibling rivalry in a single-parent family, much depends on the parent and children involved. Like most two-parent families, the vast majority of single-parent families do not present a picture of chaos, indiscipline and constant quarrelling among the children. There is no evidence from psychological research that shows children in a single-parent family are less disciplined than children in a two-parent family, perhaps because a single parent makes a conscious effort to avoid family tension.

Fathers

The role of the father has changed significantly in the past three or four decades. Boundaries between expectations of mums and dads have become blurred, and the respective parental roles have begun to blend into each other. So, for instance, dads are expected to do more around the house in terms of basic management of the children and carrying out routine household chores. And mums are expected to pull their weight financially by returning to work, often before the children reach school age. Today's father can shed the traditional expectations and become more involved with his children, if he has the necessary motivation.

This rejection of the more traditional fatherly role does not mean, however, that the typical father plays no part at all in establishing family discipline — it just means that his involvement and contribution have changed. Fathers are just as likely as mothers to advocate a style of discipline that is reasonable, flexible and responsive. Compared to previous generations, few fathers nowadays would be regarded as overly strict with their children.

There is also some evidence from psychological research which shows that when a father has a positive emotional relationship with his older child before the other children are born, then the older child usually feels less threatened by the new arrival. This has a knock-on effect of reducing sibling rivalry. So dad's greater involvement in family life certainly suits all the children.

STYLES OF PARENTAL DISCIPLINE

What sort of parent are you, when it comes to discipline? Are you very strict, ready to pounce on your children as soon as they step out of line, or are you easy-going and able to tolerate an occasional sibling squabble? Are you cold and aloof when you lay down the law, or do you give the impression that you set rules because you love your children and just want them to be settled at home? There are as many different types of discipline as there are parents, but here are some typical 'parent-discipline personality profiles'. You may recognize yourself in one – or more – of them.

The Bossy Parent

This type of parent knows best, no matter what anyone else tells her. As far as she is concerned, she decides what the standards of behaviour are at home and she is determined to make sure that her rules are followed to the letter. Nothing is negotiable; no exceptions are made. Everything is spelled out clearly for the children so that there is no confusion about what they can and cannot do. If one of the children does misbehave, punishment is swift, thorough and severe.

Effect on Sibling Rivalry

Bossy parents have bossy children. Just as the parent pushes the children about in order that they should conform to her wishes, so the children push each other about in order that their siblings conform with their wishes.

The Fair Parent

She wants discipline but she does not want to bully her children into good behaviour. She takes the approach that rules are good for her children, as long as they understand them. That is why she tells the children in advance how she thinks they should behave, and then listens if they have any reasonable objections. She is quite flexible and is prepared to turn a blind eye towards occasional minor acts of misbehaviour. Her children follow family rules because they want to please her.

Effect on Sibling Rivalry

Bickering among the children is less common with this type of parent because the children are taught the purpose of discipline, not just the rules. They are also taught to respect other people's views.

The Laid-Back Parent

Children have to learn from experience and from their own mistakes, according to this type of parent. She lets the children do as they please (as long as they do not wreck the house or seriously hurt each other) because she believes that discipline must come from within, that it should not be imposed all the time by adults. The children are raised in a loving atmosphere, but are expected to take responsibility for themselves at an early age. Freedom of choice is highly valued.

Effect on Sibling Rivalry

Children brought up in this type of environment tend to have a high level of sibling rivalry, because they are used to doing what they want. They may be more independent but they do not spend too much time thinking about others.

Whatever type of parent you are regarding discipline at home, it is probably a good strategy to avoid extremes of severity or leniency. Children appear to get on best with each other when family rules are reasonable and perceived to be fair. In addition, rivalry is less frequent when the children feel loved rather than controlled.

CONSISTENCY IS CRUCIAL

Aside from the style of discipline you use with your children, the predictability of your discipline is also important. Suppose, for instance, one of the rules you have at home is that your children are not allowed to take a fizzy drink into the living room in case they spill it on the carpet, and that you have explained this to them. Imagine how your children would feel if you only bothered about this some days but not others. They would not be able to anticipate your reaction and might become extremely indignant when you reprimanded them for bringing a fizzy drink into the room one day even though you let them do it a few days earlier. Inconsistency confuses young children, and may even make them afraid.

Your discipline can be inconsistent:

— *from one day to the next*. If so, your children will not know when you are likely to expect conformity to standards of behaviour and when you will ignore their misbehaviour. This could lead to a deterioration in their own relationships with each other.

— *from one child to the next*. If so, you might be firm with one of your children but much more flexible with one of the others. Not surprisingly, sibling rivalry ferments in this atmosphere because your children will recognize your different responses and they will become jealous.

— *from one parent to the next*. If so, you might have a rule that your partner does not bother about. Your children will realize that family discipline varies depending on which parent is at home at the time. This creates a divisive atmosphere, which in turn leads to ill-feeling between the children.

Make sure that you and your partner agree on the theory and practice of discipline at home, and that you are both prepared to be consistent in your approach. If you do have disagreements over the management of your children, try to resolve these speedily, preferably through calm discussion and compromise.

SMACKING

Most parents have smacked their child before she reaches the age of 5 – but that does not make it the right thing to do. The problem is that a pre-school child has state-of-the-art techniques for annoying her mum and dad. She intuitively knows your weak spots, such as which ornament she should not touch (because it is very special to you), which room she should not go into (because it contains storage boxes delicately balanced on top of each other), and which button she should not press (because she may switch on a potentially dangerous electric gadget).

In peak moments of anger and stress you may not have been able to resist the temptation to smack her as an immediate punishment for her annoying behaviour – parents are only human, after all. But you probably felt rotten afterwards, making a pledge that you would not lift your hand to her again . . . until the next time, that is.

Widespread surveys have shown that smacking is a regular means of discipline in some families. A significant percentage of parents smack their baby before she is 1 year old, and a large percentage smack their pre-school child up to six times a week. Popular reasons for smacking include the child placing herself in danger (such as fingers probing an electric socket), bad temper (a toddler tantrum), accidental or deliberate breakages (knocking over a fragile ornament), wilfully going against parental instructions (opening a packet of biscuits when she has been told to leave it alone), or violence (hitting a sibling or a friend). Most parents appear to smack to their child in temper, while only a few smack when they feel calm.

Smacking Influences Sibling Rivalry

Consider the following connections between smacking your children and sibling rivalry:

1. *It increases sibling rivalry by causing distrust.* A home environment in which the children are afraid to get caught misbehaving for fear of physical punishment will have a high level of tension. The children will be tempted to lie their way out of trouble, or even blame their siblings for the offence in order to escape the pain of a smack. This atmosphere weakens relationships between the children, and encourages arguments.

2. *It increases sibling rivalry by causing aggression.* Smacking is an aggressive act, no matter how you might try to justify hitting a child. And one act of aggression stimulates other acts of aggression. When your child sees that you use violence as a way of getting others to obey your rules, then she will use the same type of violence when she wants to control the behaviour of her brother or sister.

3. *It increases sibling rivalry by arousing fear.* Research findings show that fighting between siblings does not decrease when smacking is used as a punishment. One explanation

is that being hit by mum or dad makes children angrier, not calmer, and hence they squabble more with each other. Another explanation is that fear of getting smacked forces your children's fights to become secretive, sneaky and therefore to become more intense.

4. *It increases sibling rivalry by bringing about a negative atmosphere at home.* Smacking is unquestionably a physical rejection of your child. Deliberately causing your child pain runs counter to all other aspects of your parenting – there is no other time when you would deliberately set out to injure your child. It is one of the most negative actions you can take. No wonder your child feels miserable afterwards and picks a fight with her sibling.

Attention-Seeking Behaviour – Discipline Without Smacking

Kate is 5 years old; her brother Steve is 7. Each night, the two children and their mum and dad sit down to a family meal. And each night, without fail, Kate misbehaves in some way. One night she might interrupt whenever another person speaks at the table, another night she might try to push Steve off his chair, and other nights she might refuse to eat, flicking her food on to the floor or table. Her parents are totally fed up with her mealtime antics. They always warn her well in advance that she is going to get a smack if she continues to misbehave, but she does not seem bothered by this. Kate always ignores these warnings, even though she knows from past experience that her parents will hit her. Eventually, that is exactly what happens – she gets a smack on the bottom. By then, everyone is in a thoroughly bad mood and the family can look forward to another horrendous mealtime tomorrow night.

In this instance, smacking clearly is not having the desired effect. If Kate's parents thought about it objectively for a moment, they would see that smacking is not a deterrent. In fact, smacking may be adding fuel to the fire. There is every possibility that Kate actually enjoys the smack – not in itself, but the attention that goes with it. Kate's parents might have more success discouraging her disruptive behaviour at mealtimes if, for instance, they denied her attention by putting her into another room until she settled down, or by putting her to bed early that night. They could also make Kate the centre of attention at mealtimes by asking her to tell them her news from school, or about the children she played with that day – then she would not need to misbehave to get their attention.

How to Have a No-Smacking Discipline

The first step on the road to a no-smacking discipline is straightforward – **make up your mind not to use physical violence against your children**. Put the idea of smacking them out your mind, just as you do not seriously consider locking them in a dark cupboard when they misbehave. If you keep smacking as a possibility, then you will use it, that is for sure.

The second step is to **develop a range of strategies** for dealing with your children when they fight with each other or generally misbehave. This range might include verbal reprimands (a good telling-off can work wonders if it is used sparingly), deprivation of activities that your children enjoy (not going out to the park because they have misbehaved can be effective) or even simply letting them know that they have upset you (children do not mind upsetting each other but they rarely want to hurt their mum and dad).

The third step is to **give them attention when they behave well**. If you make a fuss of your children when they do not fight – and you tell them how pleased you are that they are getting on so well with each other – then they may prefer your praise and rewards for good behaviour instead of tongue lashings and punishments for misbehaviour.

SUMMARY

There are many influences on the way you discipline your children at home. Your own personality and the way you were raised affect your attitudes as a parent. Single parents have to overcome particular hurdles when providing discipline at home, such as excessive physical and emotional demands as well as having sole responsibility for decision-making. The role of fathers at home has changed in past decades – the typical father is less likely to be such a strict disciplinarian and is more likely to have a balanced and involved role within the family.

Sibling rivalry is affected by the style of discipline you use – it is best to avoid extremes, and rules should be applied consistently. Many parents are tempted to smack their children for misbehaviour, but this only increases sibling rivalry. There are other non-violent ways of managing your children, without having to resort to physical methods that intensify rivalry between them.

9

. . . . .

Helping your Children to Care

A DIFFERENT PERSPECTIVE

The chances are that you are quite prepared to give your children a telling-off when you see them fighting with each other. But do you make a deliberate effort to show them how to get on with each other, how to help each other when there is a problem, how to be kind to each other? This is probably not one of your priorities — most parents focus on sibling rivalry and negative behaviour rather than trying to help their children interact more positively. Yet you may be surprised at the impact on your children when you change your perspective.

Dimensions of Caring

It is important to know what is meant by the term 'caring', so that you can encourage your children to acquire these attributes. Psychologists distinguish between caring feelings and caring behaviour.

Caring feelings include:

- *Empathy:* The ability genuinely to experience and understand the feelings of another person, something we do not normally associate with young children. Yet a baby who cries because he sees another baby crying is showing

101

empathy; children are capable of being empathic.

- *Sympathy:* different from empathy, this is an emotional reaction to seeing another person upset. So a 4-year-old is being sympathetic when he tries to cheer up his sister who is miserable (in contrast to an empathic reaction, that is, feeling miserable himself).
- *Guilt:* This is the uncomfortable feeling your child has when he knows he has done something that is likely to make another person (such as you, his sister, his friend) unhappy. Guilt is a normal and healthy response in a child, and automatically motivates him towards more caring behaviour.

Caring behaviour includes:

- *Co-operation:* As when your children collaborate in order to achieve a target that benefits them all (such as combining their play-dough so they can build a larger model). This contrasts with competition, in which typically only one child benefits.
- *Sharing:* This type of caring behaviour takes places when one of your children gives something to his sibling, without hoping to achieve anything for himself. For instance, sharing occurs when one of your children lets his sister play with his favourite jigsaw without asking to play with her toys in return.
- *Turn-taking:* Your children cannot possibly play games together without fighting, unless they are all able to take turns. The problem is that a young child is generally concerned only with himself, and does not want to wait while others go ahead of him. Turn-taking usually has to be learned.
- *Pacifying:* Watch your children bicker with each other — you will notice that they tend to use aggressive gestures to each other, such as scowling, shouting and clenched

fists. However, there are other gestures which invite a peaceful response, such as smiling, showing approval and offering a toy.

- *Following rules:* As with turn-taking, your children cannot play positively together unless they follow rules, because rules impose a structure and pattern upon a play activity; this means each child can predict the other's behaviour. Caring interactions depend on being able to follow a common set of rules.
- *Positive reinforcement:* Just like you, your children spend more time reacting to their siblings' annoying behaviour than they do to their caring behaviour. Yet research confirms there is less sibling rivalry when children show pleasure at their sibling's sociable actions.

Your children's pro-social development is a combination of their caring feelings and their caring behaviour. If a child only has caring feelings but does not demonstrate this in his behaviour, then he will not be regarded as caring by others; similarly, if he behaves in a caring way but does not have the associated underlying feelings, then his thoughtful behaviour will not last long. Both dimensions matter.

CARING DEVELOPS IN STAGES

Each of your children has a natural instinct to be kind and loving towards other people. There is plenty of evidence – discussed in the chart below – to suggest that the ability to be caring is instinctive. True, you can help your child to develop this innate tendency so that his behaviour towards others is more positive, but the tendency is there already. The chart below lists the major stages in your child's social development.

Age	Pro-Social Characteristic
1 week	Watch your baby's reaction when he hears another baby cry – for instance when you are still in hospital with him. He will probably burst into tears as well – it is as though he knows the other baby is unhappy so he is unhappy too.
6 months	Now your infant is stimulated by any emotional reaction he witnesses in another person. That is why he will cry when he hears someone else crying, and will laugh when he hears someone else laughing. He empathizes with others.
12 months	Your child will have a worried expression on his face when he sees someone in distress. However, he remains rooted to the spot – it does not occur to him to go over that person in order to comfort her.
15 months	Now that he can walk confidently he may approach a child who is crying, but he will offer only general comfort (such as a smile) instead of offering specific help which could actually solve the problem that is causing the distress.
18 months	Your child will offer specific help to someone who is unhappy, but the help will not be appropriate and reflects his own emotional needs – so he might offer his cot blanket to a crying adult because that is what would cheer *him* up when he is crying.

2 years	When your child sees you carrying out a routine household chore, such as setting the table for dinner or tidying up, he will try to help you. Even though he is not particularly competent, his efforts to support you are genuine.
3 years	His empathy has developed to the point where he has a better awareness of the other person's perspective. So if you are sad because you have lost your purse, then your child will help you look for it.
4 – 5 years	Now that he is in school, he becomes more co-operative and more caring because much of the learning in the infant classroom takes place in groups. Through this experience he learns the importance of getting on with others.

BONDING MATTERS

Psychological research has confirmed that your children's ability to care for others also depends partly on the quality of their relationship with you. It is the quality of parent-child attachments that influences the quality of sibling attachments.

Investigators studied a group of children at two key points in their development – at 18 months and again at 4 years of age. The research programme was structured as follows:

Stage 1

The children (aged 18 months) were assessed in terms of the strength of their attachment to their mother, using 'the separation method'. With this assessment technique, each child was gently led away from his mother, and was then left to play on his own. After a few minutes the mother returned to the room where her child was, and the child's reaction on seeing his mother again was monitored closely by the investigators. On this basis each child was categorized as having either an intense bond with his mother (his face lit up when mum re-entered the room) or a weak bond (he showed only a neutral reaction).

Stage 2

The same children (now aged 4) were secretly videotaped for one hour per day during 50 free-play sessions at nursery. The researchers then scrutinized the tapes to assess how much sensitivity the children showed to others who had become distressed during the free-play sessions. Having completed this stage, the investigators then tried to discover if there were any sort of link between the intensity of the toddler–mother bond at 18 months and the level of kindness demonstrated towards others at the age of 4 years.

The results showed that the quality of the emotional connection between mother and toddler during the second year of life was related to the child's pro-social behaviour when he was a pre-schooler – children who had intense emotional attachments with their mother were more likely to care about another child's unhappiness than were children who had had weak bonds with their mother. This indicates that the relationship you have with your child is another influence on the development of his kindness and caring behaviour. Forging and maintaining a close emotional connection with your children indirectly enhances their relationships with each other, and consequently reduces sibling rivalry.

SIBLINGS HELP

You may be surprised to learn that the simple fact of having a brother or sister encourages an individual child to be more caring towards others – though this may seem a strange statement given the fighting that goes on between your children at home!

By the time your children are aged 3 or 4, they spend more time in the company of their siblings than they do with you, and these sibling relationships provide plenty of opportunities for learning loyalty, friendship and co-operation. Younger children are usually very caring towards older brothers and sisters – this effect becomes stronger as they grow older, and also when the older child acts in a similar way towards his younger sibling. In other words, your children can have a very positive influence on each other's behaviour – caring behaviour is infectious among brothers and sisters.

You can also help them become caring, right from the start. A study found that when mothers discussed their new baby's feelings and needs with their older child, then this older child was much more likely to be affectionate towards the new baby, by offering to help, to amuse him, cuddle him and so on. This trend continued years later.

Ten Tips for Encouraging Your Children to Care for Each Other

1. *Let them know how pleased you are when they act kindly towards each other.* Your approval of these supportive actions (such as helping a sibling with homework) will reinforce the behaviour, and makes your children realize that you value what they have done.
2. *If they are interested in having a small family pet, let them.* Your children will enjoy having a hamster or gerbil as a pet, and looking after one does not take much time or

107

organization. They will each have to take some responsibility, and this teaches them to think about others.

3. *Make sure your children know that their behaviour affects others.* They may not realize that what they do (such as setting the table for the family meal, emptying the rubbish into the bin outside, etc.) actually helps you. Tell them how much you appreciate their input.

4. *Suggest that they do more around the house.* It is their home too, not just yours, and you are being perfectly reasonable in asking them to play an active part. The more they help, the more they will get used to helping; eventually they will not need so much prompting from you.

5. *Ask your children to problem-solve.* For instance, explain that you have a simple problem (such as that you have 20 small boxes to shift from downstairs up to the loft), and ask how they could help to make this easier for you. This connects their caring behaviour to something practical.

6. *Think about your own level of kindness to others.* Explain to your children that, for instance, you try to help people out whenever you think it is appropriate (such as helping a blind person across the street in busy traffic). This sets a good standard on which they can base their own behaviour.

7. *Whatever amount of pocket money your children get, suggest they give some to charity.* There is no reason why a young child should not give charitable donations (even a few pence once a month). This gets them into the habit of thinking about others.

8. *Provide your children with experiences of turn-taking.* Encourage them to play board games where they all have to go in turns (but supervise them when they first play this type of game together, because they may initially have difficulty). This is good practice for your children.

9. *Show them how to resolve disagreements without fighting.* Once

they learn how to sort out a difference of opinion with a sibling without having to hit each other (that is, by discussion or compromise), their general level of caring behaviour should increase.

10. *Let your children say what they feel.* There is less chance of hurtful behaviour from a child who is able to express negative feelings through language instead of physical aggression. Encourage your children to speak out when they are upset about something – they should not bottle it up inside.

TOYS AND CARING BEHAVIOUR

Many parents become worried when they see their children running around with toy guns and toy knives in their hands. Although the children are only engaging in pretend-play, there is often the nagging doubt that somehow this might encourage them to be hostile in 'real life'. Parents worry that the habits and actions their children adopt during play may become second nature to them. In addition, young children cannot always tell fantasy from reality – if your 3-year-old were ever to get his hands on a real knife he might not realize that he could seriously harm someone with it. The combination of these factors make many parents think deeply about the type of toys their children play with, in case there is a link between aggressive games and uncaring behaviour.

In a classic study a group of psychologists decided to put this theory to the test. Their project involved dozens of young boys aged between 3 and 6. The children played in pairs for several short periods, watched over by the investigators.

During each play episode the boys were given the following alternatives:

- *Toys that encouraged them to be anti-social.* These were toys (such as play figures of army characters holding weapons, toy rifles, toy knives and toy pistols) that could only be used in play situations involving make-believe aggression. By their very nature these toys suggested hostile play behaviour.
- *Toys that were 'neutral'.* These were toys that did not require the children to interact with each other in any way whatsoever (such as a colouring book with a set of crayons, a small jigsaw puzzle), and therefore encouraged neither anti-social behaviour nor caring behaviour.
- *Toys that compelled them to help each other.* These were toys that needed two children to play together in order to be effective (such as a bag that had to be held by one child while the other threw a soft ball into it). If only one child played on his own, the toy could not be used properly.

The results of the video analysis revealed that the toys had a major effect on the boys' behaviour when they were playing – and also for some time after they had stopped playing with the toys. For example, the children were generally more hostile when they were playing with the toy weapons and army play figures; sometimes they became so absorbed in their make-believe play that a genuine fight broke out between them. The neutral toys did not have such a dramatic effect: the children usually played quietly with them and rarely spoke to their partners during that time. In contrast to the first set of toys, the third set (which encouraged children to help each other) resulted in more instances of co-operation and mutual support.

Evidence like this should not be ignored, as it suggests that you need to take an active interest in your children's toys. It is not a matter of censorship, just careful supervision. You should not ban your children from playing with toy weapons at home – if you do, they will almost certainly play with their friend's toy guns as soon as an opportunity arises. Instead, try to ensure that your children have a balanced range of toys, so that they do not become fixated on those that lead to hostility.

Games

Your children's games can have a similar influence on their behaviour. So it makes sense to encourage them to play games in which they have to work together to reach a solution, rather than games that always pitch them competitively against each other. Unfortunately, most childhood games do only have one winner, which means the other players will be disappointed and will be determined to outdo everyone else the next time. That is hardly the best foundation for a positive, caring atmosphere at home. The less tension generated by games, the less sibling rivalry once they have stopped playing.

Here are some special games that discourage sibling rivalry while encouraging your children to help each other. Each of these games is suitable for children aged 3 or 4 years upwards – in fact, you might enjoy playing them with your own friends! Remember, though, that your children might struggle at first because they are not used to this type of play activity. Initially there may be arguments because the older children may be impatient for the younger ones to learn the rules. Keep a close eye on them until the games are well underway, and emphasize that these games are for pleasure. They should be fun.

Game 1

Give your children a small blanket that just covers them all if they snuggle up close to each other. Tell your children that to win this game they have to cover themselves completely with the blanket so that they are all totally concealed by it. They will soon discover that they have to work together in order to achieve this goal. If one immediately pulls the cover round him, the others cannot, and so on. There will be squeals of delight as they try to hide themselves. You can time how long it takes for them all to be covered up, and then they can try to be quicker the next time.

Game 2

Get two old carpet tiles. Starting your children off at one side of the room, explain that they all have to cross the room to the other side, and that they can only do this by standing on the two carpet tiles. They are not allowed to stand on anything else. Again, they have to help each other to succeed; co-operation is essential in this game. The only way they can cross is for them all to stand on one tile, then to lay the next one down, then to step onto that one, then to pick up the first one, and so on. The process of building stepping stones will bring them to the other side. Again, you can time how long they take.

Playing these games together does not guarantee that the level of sibling rivalry between your children will instantly be reduced, but at least it is a start. There is no harm in using any opportunity or experience to show your children how they can care for each other, and that is far better than constantly encouraging competition. Your children will learn that they can have fun playing with each other instead of against each other, that achieving group targets are just as satisfying as achieving individual goals.

SUMMARY

Being caring means having a caring attitude and behaving in a caring way. Try to spend as much time as you can encouraging your children to be more caring towards each other – this will be time well spent, as it reduces sibling rivalry and creates a better atmosphere at home.

Most children have a natural tendency to care for each other and this develops spontaneously during the pre-school years, enhanced by a close parental relationship. However, there is a lot you can do to help, such as praising them when they are considerate, giving them opportunities to be helpful and teaching them how to share.

Your children are also affected by the toys they play with – toys associated with aggression tend to make children play aggressively towards each other. So pick your children's toys carefully. Similarly, some childhood games are competitive while others require co-operation between the players – both types of game have a place in your children's lives.

10
. . . . .

Personality

When psychologists talk of 'personality', they use the term differently from the way most people use it in everyday language. You may describe one of your children as having 'loads of personality' because she is very boisterous, likes to chat all the time, is fun-loving and enjoys the company of other people. Likewise, you may describe another of your children as having 'no personality' because she has a very quiet nature, is basically very shy, and needs you to persuade her to go to a friend's party. Psychologists, however, use the word 'personality' in a broader sense to refer to those personal characteristics in a child which appear to be long-lasting. A toddler who is shy has personality—it is just that her personality is different from that of a toddler who is very sociable.

Each of your children is an individual, with her own unique personality. And this determines how she behaves, how she gets on with you and how she gets on with her brothers and sisters. There are several different theories of personality development, all with their own emphasis and all leading to their own suggestions for reducing sibling rivalry.

PERSONALITY DEVELOPMENT: THE PSYCHOANALYTIC PERSPECTIVE

Freud believed that early experiences are the greatest influence on your child's personality development; he also believed that what happens in childhood has a permanent effect and lays the foundation for later adult life. His psychoanalytic theory claimed that every child is born with a number of instincts, such as hunger, thirst, love, aggression and self-satisfaction. In the pre-school years, a child learns to control these instincts, although many of them are simply repressed into the unconscious where they lie passively until they break through again at a later date. Freud regarded the period of childhood as a time for parents to curb their baby's selfish impulses so that she would develop into a caring, loving member of the family, able to mix positively with her brothers and sisters.

Freud also proposed that a child is affected by emotions stemming from two sources. First there are conscious feelings that the child is aware of, such as pleasure, joy, terror, anxiety and contentment. Secondly there are unconscious feelings that she does not know about. The unconscious contains any unpleasant feelings that would make the child ashamed or embarrassed if she realized she felt that way (such as jealousy towards brothers and sisters, anger towards her parents for having children other than herself, fear of being rejected by her parents in preference to her siblings). When a child is under any form of psychological or emotional pressure, her resistance is lower; this allows unconscious feelings to push through to the surface so that they begin to have a major influence on her behaviour.

For Freud, therefore, your child's personality is strongly determined by both conscious and unconscious emotions, though the unconscious has the greater effect. He was the first psychologist to maintain that a child's behaviour is always caused by a deep-rooted emotion, that nothing ever happens by chance. As far as he was concerned, even something as simple as laughter stems from an unconscious feeling.

Based on this psychoanalytic perspective on personality, here are some suggestions for reducing and resolving your children's squabbles:

- *Look for a deeper explanation of your children's behaviour.* For instance, suppose two of your children are apparently fighting over a toy. Their argument may actually be triggered by something more fundamental, such as one child's jealousy of the other's success in school, or one child's hurt at being left out of the other child's game. Think about the various possibilities and try to identify the source of your children's antagonism.
- *Encourage your children to talk about their differences.* The best way to release inner feelings — conscious or unconscious — is through discussion. Of course, young children prefer to act on their impulses rather than to voice them, but you should try to encourage them to say what they feel about each other rather than to resort to blows. This reduces their need to quarrel physically.
- *Be prepared to interpret their behaviour for them.* Your children probably will not have any idea why they bicker so much; you may have to explain things very clearly to them; for example, 'Although you've said you dislike your brother's jumper, I think you have only said that because you're annoyed he didn't want to play with him and his friends.' This type of comment helps your children understand their feelings more accurately.

THE BEHAVIOURIST PERSPECTIVE

Behaviourism is another important theory of child development. Like psychoanalysis, this theoretical view of personality acknowledges that parent–child relationships are crucial in influencing a child's progress in the early years. However, this conclusion is reached for entirely different reasons. As its name suggests, behaviourism focuses only on behaviour, and does not consider feelings and thoughts. A child's behaviour is all that matters, according to behaviourism, and all behaviour is learned by the child after she is born.

The starting point of this theory arose a century ago, when Russian psychologist Pavlov proved that a dog could be trained to salivate as a result of something other than food. By letting the dog hear the sound of a bell a few seconds before giving him a plate of food, Pavlov found that the dog quickly learned to salivate as soon as he heard the bell, without even seeing the food. Using this technique Pavlov *conditioned* the dog to behave differently. Then, one of Pavlov's students demonstrated that a young baby could be taught to salivate to a bell, just like the dog. After that, the possibilities became endless. The assumption was that if the behaviour of a primitive dog could be modified like this, then parents should be able to teach their children how to behave properly.

Some years later, B. F. Skinner found that the rate at which behaviour is learned depends on a number of factors, including the type of rewards. He established what he called 'laws of learning' – a system of rules about the process of learning. These laws of learning have led to some remarkable demonstrations. Using techniques of reward and punishment, Skinner was able to teach two pigeons to play table-tennis with each other (the bats were suspended in front of the pigeons, who were taught to strike them with their beaks at the right moment, thereby returning the ball over the net to their opponent). He also taught rats how to run through a complex maze, from start to finish, without making a single mistake.

Skinner took his theory one stage further, however. He claimed that children learn new behaviour in the same ways that animals do – in accordance with his 'laws of learning'. (Many psychologists disagree strongly with this view.) He also maintained that a child can be taught any type of behaviour, as long as she is taught in small steps, bit by bit, and as long as her successes are rewarded.

Based on this behaviourist perspective on personality, here are some suggestions for reducing and resolving your children's squabbles:

- *Reward your children when they get on well with each other.* This reinforces their good behaviour and encourages them to behave in the same way again in the future. Rewards do not have to be extravagant – just as long as they are appealing to your children. An extra few minutes' play or attention before bedtime that night, special praise from you, or even simply smiling at them can provide them with sufficient motivation.
- *Punish your children when they fight with each other.* When their sibling rivalry is followed by a punishment, your children are less likely to behave the same way in the future because they will not enjoy the outcome. Just as rewards do not have to be substantial, neither do punishments. You may find that a disapproving look or a quick verbal reprimand is enough to discourage your children from further arguments.
- *Be careful not to reward their misbehaviour inadvertently.* If the real reason your children squabble is to get your attention – and then you give them your attention – you will involuntarily encourage them to continue to misbehave. Try to ignore their minor bickering (if you can), and be careful to give your attention to the child who is not fighting with her brothers or sisters.

THE SITUATIONIST PERSPECTIVE

Another aspect to consider when understanding your children's personality development is the effect of their environment. When your children argue with each other, think about the situation in which that rivalry occurs – maybe it would stop if the situation changed. 'Situationist' psychologists claim that a child's personality changes when her surroundings change, and that there is no such thing as a permanent personality trait. They maintain that this is the reason children can, for instance, have a placid personality in the company of strangers, and yet have a dynamic personality in the company of people they know well. It all depends on the situation.

Research into this view of personality began with a study investigating children's honesty. The young children who took part in the research were placed into a series of specially-devised situations in which they knew they could be dishonest without having to worry about being detected. For instance, each child in the project was left in a room in which there were boxes containing lots of money. The child did not know that every box had been secretly marked so that the researchers knew how much cash was in each one. This meant that the child was made to believe she could steal money without being found out.

The researchers found that the personality trait of honesty changed as the child moved from one situation to the next. Some children were dishonest in many situations but not in others, while others were mainly honest but submitted to temptations on one or two occasions. According to the situationist perspective, this proves that a child's personality changes from context to context, and is not static.

Situationist psychology emphasizes that parents need to know as much as they can about what is happening in their child's life before they can hope to understand the meaning of her behaviour. A child's behaviour may be a reflection of her current circumstances, and the only way to verify this is to observe her closely in a variety of situations.

Based on this view of personality, here are some suggestions for reducing and resolving your children's squabbles:

- *Do not over-react to sibling rivalry.* No matter how terrible the fight appears, keep reminding yourself that it will not always be like this — because the fact that your children disagree with each other on some occasions does not mean they will react this way every time. Their fight could be more a function of the situation than a function of their personalities; in another part of the house or with other games, they might behave differently.

- *Look at the situation in which sibling rivalry occurs.* This is particularly relevant when you see a pattern emerging in their behaviour. For instance, if your children always cry when playing board games, there may be a situational factor influencing them. It could be that one of your children plays too aggressively, or that one of them dislikes competing with her siblings. Look closely before reaching a conclusion.

- *Try to change the situation, before trying to change your children's behaviour.* Instead of reprimanding your children for fighting, direct your efforts towards changing the situation in which their fight occurs. You may find that basic modifications (such as providing more supervision, reducing highly active games when they are tired, etc.) improve their behaviour more effectively than just reprimanding them.

BIRTH ORDER AND PERSONALITY

If you are the oldest child in your family, perhaps you remember feeling annoyed because your parents told you to be well-behaved in order to set a good example for your younger siblings. If you are a second-child, perhaps you remember being angry because relatives and teachers always compared you to your elder sibling. If you are the youngest in your family, perhaps you remember feeling hurt because you always had to go to bed first, while the others stayed up later and had so much fun without you. These feelings are convincing evidence that birth order (a child's position in her family) influences sibling rivalry.

Other evidence that birth order can be a significant influence on the way a child's personality develops comes from psychological research. A great many studies have compared children of different birth orders, and the results show clear differences between first-born children, second children, youngest children and so on.

First-Born Children

You learn a lot about being a parent from caring for your first-born child. It is all theory until that moment when she arrives – then it is time to roll up your sleeves and learn through practice. Parenting suddenly seems an overwhelming responsibility. There is so much to do straight away, such as learning how to comfort the new baby and how to keep her happy, well fed, clean and dry. You do not always know what to do, but you gradually build up your self-confidence and ability through the experience of raising your first child.

Research has found that first-born children:

- get better grades at school, are more successful in their careers and are usually brighter than their siblings
- are generally less confident than their siblings and tend to be more anxious about new experiences
- prefer to listen to other people's opinions before reaching a decision about an important matter.

Assuming you have more than one child, your first born has to adjust to her changed family circumstances when the new baby appears. She is the only child who has mum and dad all to herself for a few years, then has to get used to sharing them. All your other children have at least one sibling from the moment they draw their first breath. (This is discussed in detail in Chapter 2.)

121

Second Children

Your confidence has greatly improved when your second child is born. The couple of years experience as a parent means you can throw away your 'L-plates'; the little things that used to cause you hours of worry do not bother you at all now (such as whether she should wear the yellow socks or the green socks, or which disposable nappies are best). You are more relaxed. But you also need to get used to having two young children in the house at the same time. You are much busier than ever before, as both need your attention – their demands are never-ending.

Research has revealed that second children:

- are not as successful as they are expected to be; they do not seem to reach their full potential at school
- have a more relaxed personality, and are not so concerned about gaining achievements in life
- do not conform; they are attracted to unconventional ideas, unconventional clothes and unconventional activities.

Sibling rivalry often exists between the second child and her older sibling, particularly is she lives in the shadow of the first child's high achievements. There are few things more likely to cause tension between children in the same family than unwelcome comparisons – avoid these where possible!

Youngest Children

The effect of being the youngest child in a family depends not just on your behaviour as parents but also on the way her older siblings behave towards her. For instance, if there is a large age gap then they might spoil her and let her do what she wants. Or if there is a very small age gap, they might feel resentful and always make sure she is at the back of the queue, behind them. Try to ensure that your youngest child is treated in a fair and balanced way by others in the family.

Research has revealed that youngest children:

• are the most confident children of all the siblings; they have to learn to fight for their share of things, and this appears to strengthen their ability to cope
• tend to be extremely independent, and if they do have a problem to solve, they prefer to solve it on their own, without help from their siblings
• are usually less concerned with how they look; clothes, make-up and jewellery do not matter so much to them.

Youngest children often feel that they have a tougher time than anyone else because the older siblings have more freedom and appear to have a more exciting way of life. That is why it is worth explaining to your younger child that her siblings have less restrictions as they are older – this may be obvious to you, but not to her. Point out that she will have the same opportunities as her siblings when she is older.

Twins

Despite popular opinion, identical twins are not exactly alike. For instance, one twin will probably prefer to use her right hand while the other twin prefers to use her left. Twins also have different personalities – just because they look the same, this does not mean that they think the same way, feel the same way or act the same way. While there are instances where twins develop a special language which only they can understand, this also sometimes happens with two siblings who have a small age gap between them.

Research has revealed that twins:

- are more likely to have speech problems, although these are usually minor and can be corrected before they reach school age
- tend to be very confident, as long as they are in each other's company; they may be insecure at first when they take part in separate activities
- share easily with each other; they do not usually fight over toys and possessions as other siblings do.

Sibling rivalry can occur between twins as easily as between any two children in a family, because they are two individuals with their own needs and desires. No matter how hard parents and others might try to keep them the same, their distinctive personalities and skills will show through. Comparisons of twins are very tempting, but are unfair and unreasonable. When it comes to school arrangements, some parents prefer their twins to be split into different classes.

POSSIBILITIES OR PROBABILITIES?

Despite these research findings about birth order, and the potential sibling conflicts arising from them, you can probably think of people who do not fit these patterns of development. This confirms that nearly all the personality traits associated with different birth orders can be affected by sensitive parenting. If you are concerned that sibling rivalry in your family may be increased by the effects of birth order, then consider the following suggestions:

- *Make each of your children feel special.* Older or younger, every child needs to feel that she is as important as anyone else in the family. If one child thinks that her sibling is held in higher esteem by mum and dad, then jealousy will arise. So do your best to listen to each of your

124

children, and to respond to them positively.

- *Show enthusiasm for all your children's achievements.* You may find that you are less excited about your younger child's milestones (such as her first step, her first word, her first birthday party) than you were with your older child. It is not that you love her less, just that there is not the same novelty. If you do feel this way, do not let it show — your youngest child needs you to be interested.
- *Give each of your children responsibility.* Resist the trap of giving your oldest child all the household chores. There is no reason why she has to do everything, just because of her age. Her younger siblings can also help, for instance, by tidying toys. And the oldest child does not need to take her younger siblings with her whenever she goes outside to play.
- *Respect all your children.* Every child has the same psychological need to be loved and accepted by her parents, no matter what position she has in the family. She has feelings and ideas that she wants to express and she has a right to receive respect, to be taken seriously, whether she is the youngest, middle or oldest child.

SUMMARY

Every child is a unique individual, with her own distinctive personality, and this affects how she relates to her siblings. The main psychological theories of personality development — the psychoanalytic, behaviourist and situationist perspectives — offer different explanations of your children's personalities, and different solutions for reducing sibling rivalry.

Birth order is another influence on your children's personalities. Research findings suggest that there are clear differences between first-born, second and youngest children. However, these differences in personality are only trends, not certainties. If you are concerned that sibling rivalry may be increased by the effects of birth order, then you can take action to counter this; for instance, make each child feel special, give equal encouragement to all your children, and ensure that every child in your family shares responsibility.

11

. . . . .

Children with Special Needs

All children have similar psychological needs, such as the need to be loved by their parents, the need to be cared for and nurtured by their parents, the need to feel valued and so on. However, some children either have delayed development or atypical development, causing them to have additional special psychological needs. This could include the need for extra stimulation at home from mum and dad during the early years, the need to be encouraged to achieve independence, or perhaps the need for speech therapy if the child's development of speech and language is delayed.

Statistics confirm that the majority of children with special needs have at least one brother or sister. Understandably, a child with special needs places additional strains on every member of the family – and there is a direct effect on sibling rivalry.

INCIDENCE

There have been several surveys which have tried to establish the incidence of children with special needs, but their results have varied. For instance, one study involving thousands of children concluded that over 15 per cent of all children have problems with their progress during the pre-school years, whereas another major project found a lower incidence. The difficulty facing researchers trying to quantify the rate of special needs among the child population is that the severity of special needs varies from child to child. However, most professionals accept that between 15 and 20 per cent of children have special needs.

MAKING A GOOD START

As discussed in previous chapters, sibling rivalry usually starts around the time of the pregnancy and the birth of the new baby, and that rivalry becomes more intense if the older siblings see that their parents are struggling to cope. The existing children will resent the new baby if they think that mum and dad do not love them as much, or if mum and dad are more moody since the birth.

From your other children's point of view, therefore, it is important for you to form an emotional attachment with your baby with special needs. Here are some suggestions to help you intensify the bonds between you and your new arrival:

- *Help him play.* You may find that your baby is passive and shows few signs that he wants to play with his toys. Be prepared to start the play process off, perhaps by taking the toy to him or by placing his hands round the toy. He will benefit from this type of prompting – and you will feel more involved with him.
- *When he is upset, comfort him.* An important part of parenthood is being able to calm your baby when he is crying and upset. However, you might find this more difficult with a baby who has special needs because he may not be so responsive. Persist anyway – he will react to your efforts eventually.
- *Find out about your baby's problem.* Your confidence in caring for your baby with special needs will strengthen

when you actually know and understand about his difficulties. Ask the doctors, read information leaflets and books, and speak to other parents who have had a similar experience.

- *Do not expect too much.* Compared to other babies of the same age, your baby who has special needs may seem immature and passive. However, he needs you as much as any baby needs his parents; so play with him in a way that is suitable for his stage of progress.
- *Try to interact with him.* A baby with special needs may have limited social skills, such as poor eye contact, delayed smiling, etc. This means that he may not appear to respond to you or want to play with you. However, he does − you just have to work harder at it.

AS YOUR BABY WITH SPECIAL NEEDS GROWS

For most parents, their children become the focus of their lives right from birth − that is perfectly natural, since they want to give their children all the attention they need, to encourage them to fulfil their potential.

This focus of attention becomes more intense, however, when your child has special needs, and there are good reasons why this happens. For instance, he probably needs more stimulation in order to encourage him to progress. In addition, he may require supportive therapies such as speech therapy, physiotherapy and occupational therapy. Then there are often lots of medical appointments, more so than his brothers and sisters ever had. However, the danger is that the siblings may get left out.

Findings from psychological research show that siblings of a child with special needs:

- often experience mild emotional problems − estimates

vary, but around 10 per cent fall into this category
- experience a higher level of sibling rivalry; both verbal disputes and physical fights are more common
- tend to be more anxious; minor problems cause them more worry than would normally be expected
- often admit to their parents that they are afraid in case they have the same difficulties as their sibling who has special needs
- tend to do less well in school than would normally be expected when judged solely on the basis of their ability.

This does not mean that siblings of a child with special needs are always at risk psychologically. Some families cope better than others, and there may be positive effects (for instance, the children may become more sensitive towards each other; they may become more supportive and understanding; parents and children may experience a closer relationship with each other). Yet for many siblings the presence of a child with special needs in the family causes feelings of jealousy and rivalry. The chart below lists the main factors that intensify sibling rivalry when there is a child with special needs in the family, and explains the significance of these factors.

Factor	Significance
Too many demands	The siblings may resent being asked to do extra household chores because their parents are so involved with the child who has special needs
Feeling neglected	The siblings may feel neglected because their parents have to spend so much time caring for the child with special needs, taking him for appointments, etc.
Resentment about dependence	A child with special needs reaches independence at a later time than other

High expectations
children. His siblings may resent the additional demands this places on the family.

Parents of a child with special needs often expect too much of their other children, perhaps as compensation for the child's difficulties.

1. How to Avoid Making Unreasonable Demands

Living in a family involves thinking about others and being helpful towards them. Your children should care about their siblings and should take an interest in them – that is perfectly normal and is part of growing up. So there is nothing wrong in asking your 4-year-old to help his sister put the dirty glasses into the sink; nor is it unreasonable to ask your 5-year-old to allow another sibling to borrow his coloured pencils. Through this sort of behaviour your children become more sensitive to the needs of others.

Resentment will start to form, however, if your children feel they have no time for themselves because they are always busy doing something for someone else, or if they feel that their friends do not have to do such much in their families. Siblings of a child with special needs are more likely to feel this way. An abnormally high level of domestic responsibility will cause siblings to resent a child with special needs.

Here are ways to avoid making unreasonable demands:

- *Listen to your children's complaints.* Your first reaction might be to dismiss out of hand your children's groans about being asked to do too much. However, they may be right – listen to what they have to say, take their comments seriously, and judge whether or not they have a point.
- *Consider your children's daily schedules.* Even though your

children may not be aware of it, they may be in a position of being asked to do too much. Make sure they have enough time to play with their toys at home, and to be with their friends.

- *Share out household chores fairly.* Your oldest child does not always have to be the one who sets the dinner table because you are busy bathing your child with special needs. Your younger children should be expected to play their part around the house too.

- *Be honest with your children.* Let them know that you are aware of their feelings ('I know you don't like having to carry the shopping in from the car every day, but it means I have more time for your brother'). Comments like this acknowledge your children's feelings.

- *Give them an unexpected break.* Even when they are extremely helpful and supportive, there is no harm in announcing that they can have a day off — assuming they deserve it, of course! A special treat makes them feel more positively about the situation.

- *Explain that they are helping you, and praise them for it.* Your children may not realize the impact of their support for you, so tell them 'Your tidying up means that I can play longer with your brother, and that is going to help him learn to talk.' They will feel better having heard this explanation.

2. How to Avoid Making Them Feel Neglected

Your time is at a premium — the more children you have, the less time you have to spend with each one individually. Fortunately, children do usually adapt to this without becoming troubled. When your child has special needs, though, he needs more attention and input from you; his developmental weakness mean that he needs more help from you. That is the reality of the situation — it is not that you prefer him to your other children, just that he is more dependent than everyone else in the family.

The result of this need for extra attention from mum and dad could be that your other children feel left out; they may feel that they are less important to you. Your other children quite naturally see the situation from their own perspective. They may feel neglected, or that they are loved less than their sibling with special needs. Another common feeling in siblings of a child with special needs is that their parents only show interest in the progress of the child who has difficulties. All of these feelings can increase sibling rivalry.

Here are ways to avoid your other children feeling neglected:

- *Make time for each of your children.* Although your child with special needs takes up a lot of your time, try to arrange things so that you have a few minutes every day to talk to each of your other children on his or her own. They need this 'quality time' with you.
- *Do not focus all family activities around your child with special needs.* Let the other children choose the family weekend outing, even though their choice might not exactly suit your child with special needs. They deserve to make choices, too.
- *Take them along with you when possible.* They will probably enjoy being with you, even if they are only accompanying you and their sibling on one of his medical appointments. Your other children will enjoy having the opportunity to talk to you and to be with you whenever you and they can.
- *Demonstrate your interest in their achievements.* Make a fuss when one of your other children makes progress, such as managing to complete a difficult jigsaw. Every achievement merits your interest, not just those of your child with special needs.

- *Tell them why you have so little time.* Explain to them that you are so busy with their sibling that you have less time for them. But emphasize that you love them just as much and that you would do the same for them if they ever needed your help like this.
- *Make plans for the future.* Your children will love to plan future activities with you, whether it is a day out or a longer family holiday. Even if they feel sorry for themselves now, planning like this makes them feel involved with you, and with each other.

3. How to Avoid Resentment

Most children with special needs are slower to reach the milestones of independence than other children their own age. Basic skills such as taking that first step, saying his first word, and achieving bladder and bowel control take longer to acquire. Depending on the nature of your child's specific developmental problem, he may never acquire these skills at all. This means that he probably is dependent on you for longer than normal, and your other children may resent this.

Their attitude towards their sibling will fluctuate, however. At times they will be extremely caring and helpful, trying hard to encourage him to make progress and showing great pleasure when he does. And your child with special needs will thrive on this attention from his siblings. At other times, though, they will be annoyed with him – and possibly resent him – because his lack of independence interferes with their plans.

Here are ways to avoid your other children resenting his dependence:

- *Do not put an unnecessary burden on them.* Of course all your children should help each other, but each of your children has a right to his or her own life. Try to avoid asking too much of them, or disrupting their plans because of the demands of your child with special needs.

- *Give them knowledge of their sibling's problem.* Lack of knowledge causes distrust; the more your children understand the nature of their sibling's problem, the less likely they are to resent him – in fact, they are likely to be supportive.
- *Ask them to teach new skills to him.* Your children will take great pleasure from trying to teach him – for instance how to complete a small jigsaw, how to take his first step, or how to sing a nursery rhyme. Their active involvement in increasing his independence reduces resentment.
- *Point out that they are dependent in some ways, too.* Remind them that they too need your help at times, and that they are not entirely independent themselves. After all, they need you to run them to after-school activities, to choose their clothes, etc. This reminder need not be done in a disparaging way; the point is to show your other children that we all need help sometimes, and that there is nothing wrong with this.
- *Emphasize that he is not deliberately having difficulties.* There is no harm in telling them that their sibling has not chosen to have developmental problems; he would rather be like his brothers and sisters. Explain that his dependence, therefore, is not something he necessarily enjoys.
- *Encourage your child with special needs to be independent.* No matter what level of development he is at, there are things he can do for himself – so let him do them. You may feel very protective towards him, but he needs to do things on his own wherever possible.

4. How to Avoid Having Expectations that Are Too High

Even during the pregnancy, parents start to form ideas about what their baby will be like, and what they hope he will achieve. However, when a child has special needs he may be totally unable to attain these expectations simply because of the nature of his developmental problems. Without meaning to do so deliberately, his parents may compensate for his difficulties by having unrealistically high expectations of his brothers and sisters.

Siblings of a child with special needs sometimes feel that they are expected to be marvellous at everything, that they are expected to cope because they do not have special needs. For instance, they may feel they are expected to have no difficulties with their work in class, to have lots of friends and to play without fighting, or even to show musical talent. In addition, their parents often expect them to be perfectly 'normal' and well-behaved at all times. No wonder that sibling rivalry thrives in these circumstances.

Here are ways to avoid having extraordinary expectations for your other children:

- *Accept that each of your children is an individual.* In every family, every child is different, with his own particular strengths and weaknesses – no two children follow the same developmental path at the same rate. The fact that one of your children has special needs should not affect your view of the others.
- *Avoid the argument 'You should count yourself lucky.'* True, your other children are fortunate they do not have difficulties similar to their sibling with special needs, but that does not mean they will have no difficulties whatsoever. Reminding them of their sibling's problems does not help.

- *Do not overreact to their misbehaviour.* Your children are going to be naughty at times, as is your child with special needs. This is part of childhood, and is to be expected. The fact that they have a sibling with special needs does not mean they will always behave just as you would like them to.
- *Have expectations appropriate to your children's abilities.* There is no point in expecting your other children to make great educational achievements in school unless they have the ability to do so. You cannot make them have talents and skills just because you would like them to.
- *Analyse your own motives.* Think about the standards you set for your other children, and decide whether or not you are being reasonable. Satisfy yourself that you are not asking too much simply as a way of compensating for having a child with special needs.
- *Expect the same standards of behaviour from all your children.* Your child with special needs requires discipline as much as the others. Expect the same level of good behaviour from him as you do for his siblings – this benefits all of them.

Family Characteristics

The way your other children react to their sibling with special needs – and the degree of sibling rivalry that develops – also depends on other factors, too. For instance, **the age of the child with special needs** has an effect. A sibling who is much older than him will have known about his difficulties right from birth, and will have been involved the moment he came back from hospital. A sibling who is much younger than him will not understand her sibling's special needs until she reaches school age, and by then the seeds of resentment may have been sown.

137

The sex of the sibling has an influence. Research data suggests that girls are more likely to have a difficult emotional reaction to having a sibling with special needs than are boys, and are more likely to harbour feelings of resentment. Lastly, there is **the severity and type of the child's developmental difficulties**. When the problems are severe, the emotional impact on his siblings is more intense. In addition, children seem more able to adjust to a sibling with special needs when his difficulties are physical rather than intellectual.

ADDITIONAL GUIDELINES FOR REDUCING SIBLING RIVALRY

In addition to all the points made earlier in this chapter, here are some general guidelines to help you reduce sibling rivalry when you have a child with special needs:

- *Let them help look after their sibling.* Do not keep them at a distance from him just because he has difficulties with his development. Their relationship with him will be stronger if they can get to know him and to feel that they are an important part of his life.
- *Encourage your children to talk about their sibling's difficulties.* They may feel uncomfortable or guilty talking about the problems their sibling faces, and about the way this affects their own lives. Help create an atmosphere at home in which your children feel able to talk.
- *Accept their feelings without criticism.* At times they will feel negatively towards their sibling with special needs, even though they wish they did not. Do not add to their guilt by saying how disappointed you are that they feel this way. It is better for them to express these feelings than to hide them from you.

- *Tell them what you know about their sibling's problem.* You may be afraid of upsetting them by giving them the facts about your child's condition, but lack of knowledge may be even more frightening for them. Limited explanations are better than none at all.
- *Give them explanations that are appropriate for their age and level of understanding.* Avoid using medical jargon – this will only confuse your children. For instance, instead of saying 'he is paralysed,' say 'his legs don't work.' Keep it simple.
- *Prepare them for the outside world.* Explain to them that other people may not understand their sibling's difficulty and therefore may seem to be hostile. For example, their friends may make hurtful comments about their sibling with special needs – if your children can try to understand that remarks like this stem from their friends' lack of information, not from hostility, it may help them.

Excuses

Having a child with special needs in the family can at times be a convenient explanation for every incident of sibling rivalry. It is easy to use the child as an excuse in this way – it saves you from having to look at other alternatives for resolving family tensions.

Consider the following statements:

'My children fight all the time because of the strain caused by my child with special needs.'
'Our children's relationships with each other were so much better before our child with special needs came along.'
'There is so much to do for my child with special needs that I never have time for the others.'
'Life must be so much easier in a family where none of the children has any problems with development.'

'I think that my other children would be much happier at school and have more friends if they did not have a sibling with special needs.'
'Our other children would have a much more varied and interesting life if it were not for our child with special needs.'

If you find that you often have thoughts like these – and have them regularly – then you may be using your child with special needs as an excuse in order to avoid tackling sibling rivalry head on. Although he undoubtedly puts added strain on the family, he cannot be held responsible for every disagreement between your children. Look more closely at their relationships with each other, and less at their relationships with him.

SUMMARY

Sibling rivalry can intensify when you have a child with special needs because of the time and attention that he requires. It is important to form an emotional connection with him right from birth, or your other children may start to resent him even at that stage.

Siblings of a child with special needs often feel that too many demands are made of them, or that they are neglected. They may resent the continued dependence of their sibling with special needs, and they may also feel that their parents expect too much of them. There is a lot you can do to avoid these feelings building up, and this will help reduce sibling rivalry. The more your children understand their sibling with special needs, then the less likely they are to feel threatened by him or feel jealous of him. Make sure you do not use your child with special needs as a convenient excuse for all fights or tensions between your children.

12

. . . . .

Questions and Answers

Q. My two children are 6 and 4 years old and they fight a lot with each other. Are they going to be this way all their lives?

A. Feelings of rivalry that start off in childhood often do continue throughout adulthood – that is perfectly normal. But this does not mean these feelings will have the same effect. As your children grow older – with your help – they will learn to control sibling rivalry so that it has less impact on their relationship. They will realize that their jealousy is often irrational; they will also realize that having a brother or sister has many benefits that may only emerge after childhood (such as having someone to share feelings with, someone to offer advice, someone to listen to their problems, someone for company and so on). In adulthood most people recognize that the advantages of having a sibling grossly outweigh the disadvantages.

Q. I have noticed that my 3-year-old son gives his new sister such enthusiastic hugs that she starts to choke. Does he really mean to hurt her?

A. It is extremely unlikely that he is deliberately trying to hurt his sister. He probably loves her very much and that is why he wants to hug her so openly. Unconsciously, however, he probably feels threatened by her arrival – and although he is not aware of this deeper sense of insecurity, it is having an effect on his behaviour. The over-enthu-siastic hug is a combination of his genuine love towards his sister and his genuine perception of her as a threat.

Your son's behaviour is telling you that he is troubled and you should respond sensitively to him. Reassure him that you love him as much as you always did and spend as much time with him as you can. Of course, you must warn him that he is hurting his sister – though try not to tell him in an angry voice – and suggest he hugs her more gently. Be prepared to intervene firmly if his behaviour continues, reminding him that he is causing her pain. You will find that he eventually settles down again.

Q. How can I stop my 4-year-old girl from being dis-ruptive every time I start to breastfeed her baby brother?

A. Your daughter obviously feels very jealous when she sees you breastfeeding. And no wonder. After all, you hold the baby very close to you and he is in direct physical contact with you in a warm, nurturing experience. Her disruptive behaviour at that time is probably her attempt to draw attention away from her brother on to herself.

There are several things you can do to change the situ-ation. First, explain to her that she was breastfed when she was a baby (assuming that is true) and that she enjoyed it too, just like her brother does now. Secondly, keep her close beside you when you breastfeed. Let her watch you, perhaps even lean against you, so that she also has close physical contact with you. Thirdly, you could try ensuring that she has something enjoyable to do while you are feeding your baby; spend a few moments settling her down to a book, game or video before you actually start breastfeeding so that she will not seek attention simply out of boredom.

Q. When my children fight with each other they sometimes say such nasty things, like 'I hate you' or 'I wish you were dead', and I think this is horrible. Am I over-reacting?

A. No parent likes to hear her children making hurtful comments like that to anyone, let alone to their brothers and sisters and you are right to want to discourage them. Yet you should bear in mind that young children usually do not mean what they say when they speak in temper – they have probably seen an adult make these remarks and are only imitating behaviour that they have observed. If you let yourself become angry and make a big fuss, they may continue to say these things solely because they know how you will respond.

Having said that, however, you have to point out to them that comments of this sort are unacceptable. Once the argument is over, sit your children down calmly and explain to them that these words are very serious and hurtful; add that it is unkind to make remarks like that no matter how much they have been provoked. You may have to repeat this message many times, but they will eventually do as you ask.

Q. Since our baby was born a few weeks ago, our 3-year-old son literally has not spoken to her. He pretends she is not there. What should we do?

A. As far as your son is concerned, if he ignores his baby sister then she does not exist. This is his way of coping with the situation. Despite your feeling upset about his reaction, you should be cautious in your approach. Certainly you cannot force him to acknowledge her – if you try, he will probably become even more determined to ignore her. Aside from reassuring him that you love him and aside from spending time with him, casually talk about his sister for a moment or two every so often during your conversations with him. Mention something she has done, just enough so that he knows you are not going to ignore her too. Ask him to carry out a simple chore to help you with the baby, for instance fetching a clean nappy from the cupboard – and praise him when he helps you like this. There is no harm in giving him a small gift from his baby sister every so often. A gentle approach, combining all of these strategies, will win him round in time.

Q. How can I help my 5-year-old who started school recently? He is very upset most days because he is convinced he is not as clever as his older brother – and he is right.

A. The drive to achieve at the same level as a sibling often derives from within the child and not as a result of outside pressures. Your younger son is in a very difficult position because he wants to do at least as well as his older brother and yet he is not as capable. His expectations of himself are therefore unrealistic; he has placed himself in a no-win situation.

You can help him by encouraging him to value his own achievements – whether or not they match those of his older sibling – and by helping him set sensible targets for the future based on his current stage of development. Be honest with him. Tell him that you just want him to do his best in class, to do as well as he possibly can; explain that you do not compare him with his brother and that he should not do this either. Show an interest in everything he does in school. Try to encourage him to take up an interest that his older sibling is not involved in. Although he might always want to achieve the same school grades or exam marks as his brother, he will gradually develop confidence and pride in his own abilities.

Q. We have four children and we always have to buy any new clothes for our oldest so that one or two of the others can wear them next. Will this cause jealousy?

A. The chances are that your younger children will feel jealous at times, when they see all the new clothes going to their older sibling. However, you are doing this solely for economic reasons and you should explain this to them. Tell them that you understand they may feel sorry for themselves, that you are only doing this because it is too expensive to buy all of them new clothes every time. Of course, this explanation does not change the situation, but it may make them feel a bit better and less jealous. Make sure that the sibling who gets all the new clothes does not make a big thing of it in front of his brothers and sisters. And encourage him to take good care of the items so that they can be handed down intact to the younger ones.

Q. Whenever my 4-year-old sees me reprimand her younger brother, she joins in, telling him off as well. How can I stop her doing this?

A. Your daughter is taking advantage of your anger at her brother in order that she can vent her own anger at him too. And this is clearly unacceptable. She has to learn that reprimands for misbehaviour are your responsibility, not hers, and that your relationship with your 2-year-old is different from her relationship with him. Talk to her about this, explaining that she should not get involved, while at the same time reassuring her that your reprimand is sufficient.

Her apparent delight when her sibling is in trouble, coupled with her willingness to be involved in chastising him, suggest that there is already rivalry between them. Raising this matter with your daughter may be a sensible step forward – she clearly has some negative emotions towards her brother and you should try to establish why this has happened. The very act of discussing this with her may be sufficient to ease the tension between brother and sister.

Q. **Both our daughters are very competitive with each other, although they have a good relationship. They both want to have music lessons. Should we encourage them to take up different instruments?**

A. Assuming that they have not expressed a preference for a particular instrument at this stage, then it may be advisable to subtly suggest that, for instance, one might like to try the flute while the other tries the piano. You can justify this arrangement to your daughters on logical grounds – having different instruments means, for example, that they can play whenever they want without having to wait for the instrument to become available, that they can play duets together once they have become skilled, and so on. Certainly this would reduce possible conflict between them and eventually would provide opportunities for them to play together, supporting each other.

Q. **How can I help my son stand up for himself? He always gives in to his sister when she wants his toys, even though he seems to be unhappy about it.**

A. There are possibly two angles to this. First, you may have to boost your son's self-confidence so that he can stop being a victim. Remind him that he has nothing to be afraid of and that he should not let his sister have anything of his unless he wants her to. Pretend-play some scenes in which you act as his sister taking his toys – this will give him a chance to practise being more assertive and hopefully he will carry this over into his relationship with her.

The other angle to consider is that your son may not be as upset as you imagine. Perhaps he takes his sister's toys just as she takes his; this may be their agreed arrangement. What seems unfair to parents, on the surface, may suit the children themselves. So check it out with your son and daughter before taking action. Ask them what agreement they have reached about sharing toys. You may be surprised to find out that the situation is not as tense as you first thought.

Q. What can we do to help our 8-year-old son control his explosive temper? He gets into such a rage when his 3-year-old sister annoys him.

A. You are right to be worried about your son's rages, because at this age his anger can be hard to restrain and there is the possibility that he might accidentally hurt himself or his sister in temper. However, he is old enough to be aware of his behaviour during a tantrum; he can probably recognize the signs as soon as he begins to get angry and he probably feels very sorry about his behaviour afterwards.

The strategies suitable for managing the tantrums of a pre-schooler (avoiding provocative situations, encouraging the child to talk about his anger instead of acting on it, and so on) — are equally applicable to a school-aged child. But at this age he should also be encouraged to take some responsibility for the implementation of these strategies. For instance, tell your son that when he becomes frustrated by his younger sister he should walk away from her or tell you. Emphasize that he is old enough to take charge of his own behaviour. You might also teach him basic relaxation techniques such as sitting quietly while closing his eyes until his temper passes, or breathing steadily and slowly until he feels more relaxed.

Q. Our children do not fight with each other at all. Might they just be repressing their anger?

A. You are worrying unnecessarily. While it is theoretically possible that in fact there is strong jealousy between your children and that they are indeed repressing these negative emotions, the chances are that they simply get on well with each other. Do not look for problems that are not there – take pleasure from the knowledge that your children's relationship with each other is strong and positive.

Index

Of further interest . . .

STARTING SCHOOL

A parent's guide to preparing your child for school

Richard Woolfson

Starting school is a big step in any child's life and naturally every parent wants to give their child a head start so that his or her potential is fully maximised.

Starting School is a practical, accessible and reassuring guide for parents to help them prepare their child and themselves for that first day at school. It covers pre-school to the first year at infant school, including how to choose the right school for your child, pre-school learning, childhood development, the first day and what to do if things go wrong.

YOUR CHILD CAN BE A GENIUS

Early learning through play

Ken Adams

Early learning can be creative and fun and will help pre-school children get the best possible start in education. This tried and tested home-learning programme is full of easy ideas and activities to encourage children to develop their natural talents without pressure and to stimulate an enthusiasm for learning which will help them throughout their school years.

Ken Adams is not only a parent, he is a teacher too. His creative teaching methods and his innate belief that *every* child has a natural ability to succeed first came to public attention when his son, John, passed his maths 'A' level at the age of nine. Now he shares, in clear terms and with appealing images, his home-learning plan which will help every parent to ensure that their child can make the very best of their natural talents.

GOOD HABITS, BAD HABITS

Dr John Pearce

Habits such as sniffing and thumb-sucking can provoke strong reactions in parents. Parents can also feel guilty and wonder if they are somehow responsible for their child's bad habit, or whether the habit is an indication that something is wrong.

Other habits are an important part of everyday life: getting up in the morning, dressing, eating meals, going to bed at night and so on are all routines that are repeated day in and day out so that they become unconscious habits.

Good Habits, Bad Habits tells you how children's habits are formed and why some children are more likely to develop habits than others. The simple guidelines in this book will help you to develop your child's good habits and deal with the so called bad ones that can cause you and your child so much embarrassment and distress.

Dr John Pearce has over 20 years' experience as a child psychiatrist.

GROWTH AND DEVELOPMENT

Dr John Pearce

All parents are interested in their child's emotional, physical and intellectual development.

Growth and Development outlines the stages your child will go through, to reassure and help you to understand your child's unique progress from birth to adolescence.

Taking a look at what influences individual child development, this book covers a wide range of experiences, including:

- The first years of life – developing self-awareness and self-esteem
- The school years – learning how to relate to others, understanding abstract concepts and creative and artistic ability
- Adolescence – learning to cope emotionally and physically with approaching adulthood

In addition to the main stages of development, John Pearce provides information on problem areas such as reading difficulties or bedwetting which may be causing concern.

FIGHTING, TEASING AND BULLYING

Dr John Pearce

There are few things more frightening to a child than being the victim of bullying, whether by adults or other children – but many go on for months, suffering in silence.

If your child is a victim of bullying, or finds it difficult to control his or her own aggressive behaviour, John Pearce's book will help you to recognise this and offers useful strategies to help your child to learn self-control, develop confidence and improve self-esteem.

He explains:

- The differences between fighting, teasing and bullying
- How to tell when your child is being bullied – and what to do about it
- Strategies to help your child to cope
- How to 'toughen up' your child against teasing
- What to do if *your* child teases, fights or is a bully
- How to cope with bullying in the family
- When to worry about siblings fighting – and how to help your children be happy.

BAD BEHAVIOUR, TANTRUMS AND TEMPERS

Dr John Pearce

If your little darling has become a little horror, Dr John Pearce could hold the key to happier parenting:

Bad behaviour:

- What makes a child naughty?
- How can you teach your child good from bad?
- What are the best methods of discipline?
- What is the best way to deal with swearing, lying or hyper-activity?

Tantrums and tempers:

- How can you help your child cope with aggression?
- What can you do when *you* get angry?
- How to cope if a child holds its breath or sulks.
- How to avoid the things that cause tantrums.

Here are simple, practical and realistic solutions to common problems based on years of experience. Whether your child is two, a teenager or somewhere in between, you'll find something to help you in this book.

WORRIES AND FEARS

*How to help your child to cope with fears
and develop self-confidence*

Dr John Pearce

The world as seen through a child's eyes can be a frightening place. This book will help you to help your child to resolve their anxieties and gain self-confidence.

- What can you do if your child is frightened of the dark or has other night-time fears?
- How can you help your child cope with the fear of going to school, making friends, doing exams, going to the dentist?
- When does a fear become a phobia? And how do they develop?
- How can you prevent your own anxieties passing to your children?

Dr John Pearce answers these questions and more. In an easy, accessible style he draws on years of experience to help you to make your child's world a happier place.

STARTING SCHOOL	0 7225 3100 1	£4.99	☐
YOUR CHILD CAN BE A GENIUS	0 7225 3116 8	£4.99	☐
GOOD HABITS, BAD HABITS	0 7225 2296 7	£4.99	☐
GROWTH AND DEVELOPMENT	0 7225 1724 6	£4.99	☐
FIGHTING, TEASING AND BULLYING	0 7225 1722 X	£3.99	☐
BAD BEHAVIOUR, TANTRUMS AND TEMPERS	0 7225 2818 3	£3.99	☐
WORRIES AND FEARS	0 7225 1893 5	£3.99	☐

All these books are available from your local bookseller or can be ordered direct from the publishers.

To order direct just tick the titles you want and fill in the form below:

Name: _____

Address: _____

_____

_____ Postcode: _____

Send to: Thorsons Mail Order, Dept 3, HarperCollins*Publishers*, Westerhill Road, Bishopbriggs, Glasgow G64 2QT.
Please enclose a cheque or postal order or your authority to debit your Visa/Access account —

Credit card no: _____

Expiry date: _____

Signature: _____

— to the value of the cover price plus:
UK & BFPO: Add £1.00 for the first book and 25p for each additional book ordered.
Overseas orders including Eire: Please add £2.95 service charge. Books will be sent by surface mail but quotes for airmail despatches will be given on request.

24 HOUR TELEPHONE ORDERING SERVICE FOR ACCESS/VISA CARDHOLDERS — TEL: 0141 772 2281.